Barry Cameron has been anointed by God in a wonderful and unique ministry: teaching Christians and churches the Scriptural principles of finance. Barry's new book, *Contagious Generosity*, has the potential to be a best seller. As I read it, I kept thinking, "This is so valuable, I wish every Christian in our church would read it—no, every Christian in the nation! If these principles were followed, they would transform and energize the church in America, bringing revival, evangelism and compassion, and the body of Christ would no longer be a slumbering giant."

Dr. Rick Stedman, Senior Pastor
Adventure Christian Church, Sacramento, CA

If you were blessed by Barry's first book, *The ABC's of Financial Success*, you'll be blessed even more by *Contagious Generosity*. His new book takes giving to another level beyond tithing. It is only when we understand generosity that we will truly begin to receive the blessings of God. This book is very practical and the principles of stewardship Barry shares will be life changing for every person who applies them.

Dr. Don Wilson, Senior Pastor
Christ's Church of the Valley, Peoria, Arizona

Wow! What a great book! Barry Cameron has given us, in *Contagious Generosity*, a clarion call to discover the joy and fulfillment of becoming and being God's agents of blessing to others. If you want to be blessed, read this book. If you want to bless others, read this book. If you want your heart to beat with the heartbeat of God, read this book. I highly recommend it!

Dr. Ron Carlson, President
Christian Ministries International

My friend Barry Cameron excites me about giving. Every movement has its passionate spokesman: Bill Bright for discipleship; Rick Warren for living on purpose; Bill Hybels for reaching seekers; Ed Young for communicating creatively. Barry Cameron is the spokesman for contagious generosity.

John A. Hampton, Senior Pastor
First Christian Church, Canton, Ohio

Do you want a life filled with more joy and fulfillment than you can imagine? If so, turn off the TV and read *Contagious Generosity*. Barry Cameron shows the path to outrageous joy and fulfillment with wisdom and humor. Get ready to be surprised, challenged, and inspired. Practicing these principles will not only change your life, but change our world for the better.

Jud Wilhite, Senior Pastor
Central Christian Church, Henderson, Nevada

Barry Cameron's first book, *The ABC's of Financial Success* continues to have a profound impact on the Kingdom. We gave a copy of his book to every family at our church, and continue to hear countless testimonies of changed lives, not to mention the fact giving went up substantially. *Contagious Generosity* goes a step further. It challenges believers to give above and beyond the tithe — to give freely from hearts full of gratitude, love, and grace. Written in a simple, compelling style, I believe *Contagious Generosity*'s impact will exceed that of *The ABC's of Financial Success*. We'll certainly be giving a copy to every family at CFC, and can only imagine what could happen if God's people catch the contagious spirit of generosity!

Kent Williams, Senior Pastor
Christian Fellowship Church, Ashburn, Virginia

This book makes clear what too many Christians are fuzzy about: that being generous is not an option for the gifted few, but a responsibility and privilege for all who would be Godlike. Our God is a generous God, and He blesses His children when they intentionally choose to be like their Father. We need this book. The church today needs this important reminder, just as the world needs more generous Christians!

Rick Atchley, Senior Minister
Richland Hills Church of Christ, Ft. Worth, Texas

The biblical principles that Barry Cameron shared in his book *The ABC's of Financial Success* had life-transforming impact on many people in our congregation, including my own. So, when I heard that Barry was writing another book on *Contagious Generosity*, I could not wait to read it. Through the insightful teaching, intriguing stories, and personal testimonies he shares about generosity, I found it really was contagious and created in me an infectious enthusiasm to become increasingly generous in the way I handle the possessions God has entrusted to my care. Every Christian who desires to experience the fullness of God's blessing in their life will want to read this book!

Todd Hudson, Senior Pastor
Southeast Christian Church, Denver, Colorado

The curse of our day is self-absorption. The cure is generosity. In this book, Barry Cameron casts a compelling vision of what every one of us and every one of our churches are capable of becoming and accomplishing when we embrace generosity. *Contagious Generosity* explains the subject in such a way that once you get it, you can't keep it to yourself!

Cal Jernigan, Senior Pastor
Central Christian Church of the East Valley, Mesa, AZ

From his early days as a student at Ozark Christian College, Barry Cameron has been a passionate and articulate communicator. His gifts as a preacher and writer are laced into every chapter of *Contagious Generosity*. Herein is unpacked and impressed a thoroughly biblical principle that has had very little press through the years. Yet, the application of its truth in the experience of Christians and churches will produce robust spiritual health and rare spiritual dynamism.

Ken Idleman, Chancellor
Ozark Christian College, Joplin, Missouri

In advertising, the best spokespeople are the ones who believe in the product because they've experienced the benefits of it for themselves. And others can see the difference. When it comes to biblical stewardship, Barry Cameron's life speaks as clearly as his message. This resource you have in your hands is Christ-centered, engaging, insightful, and practical. It's one of the best "on-ramps" I know when it comes to getting on the highway of contagious generosity and accelerating into the blessings of God.

Chris Seidman, Senior Minister
Farmers Branch Church of Christ, Dallas, Texas

This book will set people on fire for giving above and beyond the tithe. Barry's contagious enthusiasm and passion for this subject has been changing lives all across America. Our team at Church Development Fund, Inc. has partnered with Barry to host ABC's Weekends all over the United States and the results have been beyond phenomenal. In the two years of partnership we helped thousands start down the road of debt-free living, increased church weekly giving by over 45%, helped fund numerous church buildings and facilities, and helped churches and their members plan for the future. This new book will exponentially change the church's opinion on teaching and preaching about money. God has and will continue to bless Barry's ministry as it is reaching thousands, changing lives, funding Kingdom work and establishing a solid foundation for biblical stewardship.

Douglas J. Crozier, President
Church Development Fund, Inc., Irvine, CA

"Contagious Generosity" is a concept that could leave a generational impact. Barry Cameron shares life-changing principles that will transform any home, church or work environment. As we graft with the heart of God, generosity flows from our days! These axioms for life take us beyond good intentions. The joy of giving is revived in these pages. I'm encouraged by the contagious spirit of God's character. As a participant in His Divine nature, we can become conduits of His Giving Life!

Russell Johnson, Senior Pastor
Fairfield Christian Church, Lancaster, Ohio

Barry Cameron has the rare ability to convict and inspire people on the toughest of issues. His heart is to see the Christian blessed and the world reached. He shares how these things are intertwined effectively. I love that Barry wants to see churches become change agents in their communities, as they are able to minister because of their generosity. If churches will get a hold of this, they will be able to effect change in the un-churched world because of their service and mercy, and they will be able to care for hurting Christians in their own gatherings. I pray that through this book God will strengthen His church for the mission, and that individual Christians will be a light to the world.

Jim Putman, Senior Pastor
Real Life Ministries, Post Falls, Idaho

Books about finances are not something that get me excited. Which is why *Contagious Generosity* is so compelling. Because, it's not a book about finances. It's a book about the human Heart. Barry has hit on the one thing you and I need to understand: we were created to be generous like our God and we have no choice but to follow His example. Read this book and discover how to be more like God. Then—go buy your friends a Mocha!

Drew Sherman, Senior Pastor
Highland Meadows Christian Church, Colleyville, Texas

"He who refreshes others will himself be refreshed" (Proverbs 11:25), and *Contagious Generosity* is a refreshing book. I'm glad Barry Cameron keeps challenging the church to produce more fruit for the Lord. In a self-centered age, we need to hear Jesus' countercultural observation that it's more blessed to give than to receive. This book boldly calls us to become the most generous people we can possibly be.

David Faust, President
Cincinnati Christian University, Cincinnati, Ohio

Contagious Generosity

ucial Freedom

Contagious Generosity

The Key to Continuous Blessing!

BARRY L. CAMERON
Foreword by Dave Stone

COLLEGE PRESS PUBLISHING · JOPLIN, MISSOURI

CONTAGIOUS GENEROSITY:

The Key To Continuous Blessing!

5th Printing 2011

Copyright © 2011 by Barry L. Cameron

Published by College Press Publishing Company

Scripture quotations, unless otherwise indicated, are from the Holy Bible: New International Version. NIV. Copyright © 1973,1984 by International Bible Society, used by permission of Zondervan Publishing House. All rights reserved.

Scripture quotations marked KJV are taken from the *Holy Bible*, King James Version.

Library of Congress Cataloging-in-Publication Data

Cameron, Barry L. (Barry Lee), 1955–
    Contagious generosity : the key to continuous blessing / by Barry L. Cameron.
          p.   cm.
    ISBN 978-0-89900-944-5 (softback)
    1. Generosity—Religious aspects—Christianity.   I. Title.
    BV4647.G45C36 2006
    241'.4—dc22
                                                              2006017181

"One man gives freely,
yet gains even more;
another withholds unduly,
but comes to poverty."
Proverbs 11:24

"A generous man
will prosper;
he who refreshes others
will himself be refreshed."
Proverbs 11:25

To
Wayne Smith

Friend, mentor, encourager, example.
Pastor, leader, lover of people
(especially preachers).
Thank you for showing the world what
contagious generosity is supposed to look like.

ACKNOWLEDGMENTS

I want to thank my family for their generosity in allowing me the time and space to get these thoughts and ideas on paper. I also want to thank my church family, Crossroads Christian Church, a fellowship of unstoppable followers of Christ, who are committed to being the most generous church in America. Thank you also to my fellow elders who allow me to travel to other churches and spread the germs of generosity we've all caught.

Thank you to my assistant, Vicki Dietz, who, for over two decades, has made me look much better than I really am with her multifaceted gifts and abilities. Thanks also to my editorial assistant, Erica Dietz, for helping us get the book in its final form.

Thanks to my staff for carrying on the great work God has given us, allowing me the freedom and peace of mind to be gone, sharing with other churches, knowing our ministry will continue to grow and thrive even in my absence.

Thanks again to my friends at HeartSpring Publishing, especially my editor and friend, Dru Ashwell.

Thanks to all the churches and people who have shared in the phenomenon called *The ABC's of Financial Success* and the *ABC's Weekends*! What a thrill to watch God "open the floodgates of Heaven" on local churches and individual Christians all over America!

The best is yet to come!

TABLE OF CONTENTS
Contagious Generosity

Foreword

couldn't sleep that night. Not sure why—it could have been stress or it could have been the three glasses of caffeinated sweet tea I drank late that evening. Who knows? But at about 2 a.m. I stopped tossing and turning, got out of bed, and grabbed the final manuscript of *Contagious Generosity* while I settled into a comfortable chair.

No offense, Barry, but books without pictures always tend to make me a little drowsy—especially after midnight! My hope was to read a chapter and, as fatigue set in, to slowly crawl off to sleep and drift into *shuteye utopia*.

But no such luck. My tossing and turning continued. As Barry was *tossing* out ideas, I was *turning* the pages and learning from his lifelong learnings on the topic of giving.

In case you weren't aware, some Christians are quite skittish about the topic of giving! I appreciate the forthright yet gentle way in which Barry shares the truth. It bolsters one's confidence to know that God's Word has so much to say on the subject. When you give generously your example is contagious and motivates others to take your lead and share cheerfully with others.

Money and giving are explosive topics for people, and yet there is a desire to read what others think on the subject.

Fortunately, in this case the reader will be exposed to God's teaching and not man's opinion. *Contagious Generosity* applies to your everyday life and your weekly paycheck.

This is easy reading and practical stuff—straight from the Bible. No wonder it's sensible and relevant! Several years ago I mentioned to someone, "I think Barry Cameron may be the only person I know who actually enjoys preaching on giving." But the more I've read his writings and gotten to know him, I've realized *why* he loves to write and talk on giving—it's obvious—he loves to give. God put that passion within Barry, and he is trying to teach and share what the Bible teaches on the subject.

. . . Pastors will find illustrations and scriptural substantiation for writing their next sermon on stewardship.

. . . Christians will be reminded of the blessings and joy that come from faithfully giving back to God.

. . . And everyone will find practical advice and biblical backing for why it's more blessed to give than to receive.

We never look more like God than when we give. For God so loved the world that He gave. Barry Cameron lives what he writes and practices what he preaches. My prayer is that as you read this book you will be infected with the same disease of generous giving.

Dave Stone
Senior Pastor, Southeast Christian Church
Louisville, Kentucky

INTRODUCTION

The owner of a drive-through coffee business in southwest Portland, Oregon, was surprised one morning to have one of her customers not only pay for her own mocha, but also for the mocha of the person in the car behind her. It put a smile on the owner's face to tell the next customer her drink had already been paid for.

The second customer was so surprised and blessed that someone else had purchased her coffee that she bought coffee for the next customer. As unbelievable as it seems, this string of kindness and generosity—one stranger paying for the mocha of the next customer—continued for two hours and twenty-seven customers.

Does that story inspire you? It inspires me and motivates me to be generous. Generosity is an incredible experience when you are the beneficiary of it. But it's even more incredible when you are the initiator of it. Do you know why? Because, when we are generous, we are more like God. That's why it feels so good whenever we do it. Whenever and wherever we are generous, it always feels good, always feels right, and rightly so. That's the way generosity is. Generosity reflects the character of God.

When we are generous, we are more like God. Generosity reflects the character of God.

The greatest feeling of all comes when we are generous with God and His Kingdom. Here's why. When we are generous with God and His Kingdom, we're not just giving cups of coffee to total strangers; we're helping make a difference in people's lives that will have ramifications for all eternity.

When you and I are generous with God, besides being a blessing to others, God promises to bless us generously and abundantly beyond what we can ask or think. Jesus said, "Give, and it will be given to you. A good measure, pressed down, shaken together and running over, will be poured into your lap. For with the measure you use, it will be measured to you" (Luke 6:38).

In Ephesians 3:20, Paul says, "Now to him who is able to do immeasurably more than all we ask or imagine, according to his power that is at work within us. . . ." Paul also said God promises to bless us so much that we can be generous on every occasion. "Now he who supplies seed to the sower and bread for food will also supply and increase your store of seed and will enlarge the harvest of your righteousness. You will be made rich in every way so that you can be generous on every occasion, and through us your generosity will result in thanksgiving to God" (2 Corinthians 9:10-11).

My goal is to encourage you, and thousands of others like you, to become the most generous person you can possibly be—both in giving generously to others, and in giving generously to God and His Kingdom. We won't know until we get to Heaven how many lives were changed or how huge the impact of our generosity was. But I can promise you, if you are faithful in being generous all the time, every day, every week, and every year for *The impact of your* the rest of your life, the impact and *generosity will be* influence of your generosity is going to *felt for all eternity.* be colossal. It will impact a whole lot more than twenty-seven customers in a coffee shop and will last a lot longer than two hours. In fact, the impact of your generosity will be felt for all eternity.

There's no evidence our Lord ever drank coffee. But He can identify with the generosity of the mocha drinkers in Portland. How do I know? Because He said, "It is more blessed to give than it is to receive" (Acts 20:35).

One day, over 2,000 years ago, Jesus purchased the redemption of every person who would come after Him. That one act of supreme generosity brought a smile to the Owner (God) and salvation to the world.

I'm challenging you to become a generous person. Today and every day for the rest of your life, I'm encouraging you to become the most generous person you can possibly be. Why? Because together, by being generous, we can change the world.

Will you accept the challenge?

Generosity is contagious! It's also the key to continuous blessing, as you're about to discover in the pages ahead.

Barry L. Cameron, 2006
Grand Prairie, Texas

"The wicked borrow and do not repay,
but the righteous give *generously*;
those the LORD blesses will inherit the land,
but those he curses will be cut off.
If the LORD delights in a man's way, he makes his steps firm;
though he stumble, he will not fall,
for the LORD upholds him with his hand.
I was young and now I am old,
yet I have never seen the righteous forsaken
or their children begging bread.
They are always *generous* and lend freely;
their children will be blessed.
Turn from evil and do good;
then you will dwell in the land forever.
For the LORD loves the just and will not forsake his faithful ones.
They will be protected forever,
but the offspring of the wicked will be cut off;
the righteous will inherit the land and dwell in it forever."

Psalm 37:21-29

CHAPTER ONE

Contagious Generosity
THE EXPLANATION OF IT

enerosity is contagious! Several years ago, thanks to the generosity of some dear friends, I was privileged to stay at an historic, world-class, 3,000-acre resort in Colorado Springs, Colorado, called *The Broadmoor*. Its breathtaking, Italian Renaissance styled buildings and grounds are nestled at the base of Cheyenne Mountain, with the picture-perfect backdrop of the Rocky Mountains and Pike's Peak. We had flown in from Texas, and when we checked in, the suite our friends had reserved wasn't available because people were still in it. No problem for the folks at the Broadmoor. They generously upgraded us to a larger suite. We checked into our rooms and I stood on the balcony of our room, soaking it all in, staring in awe at the most gorgeous scenery I had ever seen in my life. I was more in awe that, thanks to our friends, we were the recipients of such unbelievable generosity and my experience with the generosity of the Broadmoor was just beginning.

A few minutes later, as I tried to unpack my suitcase, I discovered the baggage handlers at the airport had evidently messed up the lock on my bag and there was no way I was going to get it open. I looked in the phone book for a local business that carried my suitcase. The closest one was about an hour a way in another town. I phoned my friend, and he told me to call the concierge to see if he could help me. Sure enough, the voice on the phone told me to leave my bag in the room and he would handle it.

We left to do some sightseeing. When we returned, my bag was open on the bed with a note from the concierge thanking me for giving him the privilege to help me. When I called to offer to pay for this kindness he told me again, it was his privilege to help and to call if there was anything else I needed. Later on I inquired to find out what had been done to get my bag fixed and learned the concierge had sent someone to the luggage dealer we had seen in the phone book in another town. I was blown away by their generosity and still am.

My wife and I were overwhelmed by the generosity of our friends and the generosity of the Broadmoor. So, a few years later, when we had paid off the mortgage on our home and gotten out of debt, we invited two more of our friends to go with us to the Broadmoor. We told them we would pay for everything, including plane flights, rooms, and rental car. This time they would be the recipients of our generosity. It was an incredible experience for all of us and reinforced the principle that "it is more blessed to give than it is to receive" (Acts 20:35), because we received a greater blessing from giving generously to our friends than we did being the recipients of others' generosity to us. My wife and I have made it a regular habit to try to go to the Broadmoor at least once a year. In fact, the idea for this book and the initial chapters were written while we were staying at the Broadmoor.

Generosity is always contagious and is supposed to be a normal way of life for all of us. Not just an occasional experience reserved for those who visit a nice resort. How do I know? Because that's the way the Creator of the Universe designed us, and everything in our world—to be generous.

Generosity is always contagious and is supposed to be a normal way of life for all of us.

You and I weren't created to keep anything. We were created to give and to give generously. However, every study conducted concerning the giving habits of people in our world comes back with the same results: we're experts at keeping, but novices when it comes to giving. An article in the *New York Times* (December, 2005) had the headline: "Study Shows the Superrich Are Not the Most Generous." The article stated that the more money we make, the less generous we are.[1] Respected Christian research expert, George Barna, says that even though evangelical Christians are among the most generous givers of all, less than 10% of them tithe to their local church.[2]

What does all that tell us? It means we're great keepers, but not so great givers. All of us. And the shocking reality is that those of us inside the church apparently struggle just as much with selfishness as our unchurched counterparts. Embarrassing as it may be, research clearly shows the contemporary evangelical community, as a whole, is not good at giving. And you really can't call us generous.

Do you see the problem? God does. After all, He created us. You and I weren't created to keep anything. We were created to give—everything.

Hold It.

Don't believe me? Try keeping your next breath. You weren't created to keep it. You were created to give it. If you don't believe me, just try to keep it. You can't. Go ahead and hold your next breath. Try to keep it. I'll wait on you. While you're doing that, look at your watch and count the seconds as it becomes uncomfortable.

How did I know you were going to start feeling uncomfortable holding your breath? Because you weren't created to keep it. None of us were. You were created to receive that breath and then to give it back—you were not created to keep it. You and I weren't created to keep anything. We were created to give. We were created not just to give, but also to be generous with everything—including the air we breathe. God never intended for any of us to be keepers. He created us to give, and to give generously.

God never intended for any of us to be keepers. He created us to give, and to give generously.

Now, if you or someone else decides no matter what anyone else says, you're going to keep your next breath, do you understand what will eventually happen? In fact, "eventually" won't be very long in coming. It will be more like four to six minutes at the max. If you attempt to hold that breath and don't give it back—you'll die. Know why? Because you weren't created to keep it. You were created to give. When you keep instead of giving, you are going to die. It's inevitable. It's inescapable.

The Creator of the universe, Almighty God, created everything in the universe (which includes you and me) to give and not to keep, to be generous and not selfish.

Let me share with you an incredible principle right up front: selfishness is destructive and deadly. It always maims, always steals, always kills, and always destroys. Always. On the other hand, generosity always blesses, always increases, always brings life, and always brings abundance. Always. That's why God created everything to give and not to keep. He's a God of giving, a God of life, and a God of continuous blessing.

So if you want to be blessed continuously, what do you think you need to do? Give and give generously. Generous giving, like generous breathing, will always bring continuous blessing—the blessing of life. Trying to keep instead (like trying to hold your breath) won't lengthen or strengthen your life. Quite the opposite, keeping always leads to death. Keeping actually takes blessings away from us, while giving brings blessings to us. It's counterintuitive, as many of the most life-transforming spiritual principles are.

In Luke 9:24, Jesus said, "For whoever wants to save his life will lose it, but whoever loses his life for me will save it." In Matthew 20:26, He said, "Whoever wants to become great among you must be your servant." In His most famous sermon, the Sermon on the Mount, Jesus told His disciples to "love your enemies and pray for those who persecute you" (Matthew 5:44).

Take a drink.

Here's another test for you. Take a glass of water and take a drink. In fact, drink all the water in the glass. Now, here's your assignment: try to keep it. Okay, I'll admit you can keep the water longer than you did the breath you tried to keep. But even though you can go several hours and maybe even a day or two, eventually you won't be able to keep that drink of water. Know why? Because you weren't designed to keep it. God designed you and me to receive a drink of water and enjoy it. One drink can nourish our thirst and satisfy us. But the satisfaction is temporary because God didn't create us to keep it. In a matter of hours, sometimes only minutes, we'll be thirsty again. Our body takes the water in and then passes the water out. Our needs are met in the process, but we are not allowed to keep the water. Why? **Because we weren't created to be keepers. We were created to be givers.**

Now, I want to stretch your brain a little. Do you realize that since the original seven days of creation, God has not created anything new? Check it out, and you'll find it to be true. God did all of His creative work in those six consecutive days and then, on the seventh day, He rested. What that means is that God created all the air the world would ever need and all the water the world would ever need in those six days of creation. That means you and I and every person who has ever lived on this earth have been breathing the same air and drinking the same water God created during those original six days of creation. God was the One Who came up with recycling. Long before man ever came up

with those green recycling containers, God had already ini-
tiated the world's first and foremost recycling program.

Now you can understand why God created us the way
He did. He created us to be generous and to be givers rather
than keepers. If those who lived before us had been keepers
instead of givers, you and I wouldn't have any air to breathe
or any water to drink. Think about that for a moment. All of us
are absolutely and completely codependent on the generosity
of others to live. God designed the universe and placed
resources there that could be used over and over again. That's
why they're called re-sources. Wow! Do you understand the
implications of that statement? If others weren't willing to
share with us and be generous
with basic necessities like air
and water, we couldn't live.
Likewise, if you and I are unwill-
ing to be generous and share
with others, others will inevitably
die as well.

> *All of us are absolutely
> and completely co-
> dependent on the
> generosity of others to live.*

Let me give you another example. Remember the last
restaurant where you ate? Do you realize that restaurant and
every other restaurant on earth was built to be generous and
to give but never to keep? Granted, God didn't create those
restaurants, men did. But the principle of contagious generosity is built into every fiber of our universe, even our eating
establishments. For instance, every restaurant on the earth
receives food and gives food. That's why they're in business.
They are not in business to keep food. If they try to keep it,
they'll go out of business. The owner would go broke
because he's in business to give.

I am fully aware it sounds weird when you read it. But it's true. That's how a restaurant owner makes money—by giving. He doesn't make a dime by keeping. If he doesn't provide food for his customers, he won't have any customers, certainly no paying customers. But it goes way beyond that.

For example, if that restaurant receives a delivery of fresh bread and they decide they want to keep the bread instead of give it, what will happen? Instead of giving fresh bread to their customers who come in to eat, if they decide they want to keep that bread on the shelves, what do you think will happen to that bread? You're already ahead of me, aren't you? That bread is going to spoil, mold, and rot until it becomes obvious to everyone it has to be thrown away. Who in their right mind would keep perfectly good bread on a shelf, until it becomes no good for anyone, including the person who made the decision to keep it?

In case you ever wondered why there are dates on boxes of cereal and crackers, bottles of orange juice and milk, cartons of butter and jars of mayonnaise, the reason is simple. If those items are kept beyond the date stamped on the package or container, they start to go bad and are of no use to anyone. In fact, the consumption of any of those items beyond the date given would be very unwise and could quite possibly be hazardous to your health.

You've probably heard the phrase "shelf life" used in reference to food. Truth is, the phrase is actually contradictory. Nothing has a shelf life. If something stays on a shelf, it's already dying. It would be more accurate to speak of the "shelf death" of things rather than their "shelf life." Every item in a grocery store or restaurant is designed to be given, not kept. Whether you're talking about grocery stores, restaurants, or even cars, the principle of contagious generosity is built into every aspect of our universe.

> *Whether you're talking about grocery stores, restaurants, or even cars, the principle of contagious generosity is built into every aspect of our universe.*

Driving home the point.

Let's talk about your automobile for a moment. Have you ever stopped to think that your primary means of transportation was designed around the principle of contagious generosity? If it weren't, the automakers couldn't sell it, and no one would ever buy it. The very fact your automobile practices contagious generosity is one of the main reasons you are paying so much money for it.

Remember the breath we talked about earlier and the drink of water? Your car is designed just like your body: built to give and to receive. It has to practice contagious generosity or you'll get rid of it. When it is unable to give any longer, it becomes useless to you and suddenly you are motivated to trade it in or sell it so you can get a car that will do what your previous one used to do.

We buy automobiles with engines that provide us with power. We like to put our foot on the gas and go. Fast. Like astronauts from NASA, we want lift off when we put our foot down. But in order for that engine to give us what we need (and want), we have to put gas in the tank and oil in the engine. Now your car can't keep that gas (wouldn't it be nice if it could?), and it can't keep that oil. What it does is use that gas and oil to meet its needs. But it also gives in generous fashion so the engine can hum and perform like a lean, mean, racing machine. Once the gas and oil are gone, we have to replace it, regularly and religiously. If we do, our automobile can keep giving generously for a long time. If we neglect to put fresh oil and gas into our automobile, it's only a matter of time before we have to get another one.

When we go out on a cold winter morning and put the key in the ignition, we want that car to give, generously. When we are leaving work after a long hard day and open the door to our vehicle and get in, we want that car to start up and give, generously, so we can go home. You could say we are dependent on the generosity of that automobile. It's also true our automobile depends on our generosity to give us what we want. See the cycle of giving and generosity? You're going to discover the principle of contagious generosity is built into every fiber of our universe, including our automobiles.

Sit back and think about this.

Giving and receiving is intricately woven into the fabric of everything in our universe. Let me give you another example. Take that chair you are sitting on. Do you realize that chair was designed to give and not to keep? It wasn't built to sit in a warehouse somewhere. That chair was built to sit in your house or someone else's, an office complex, business, school, church, you name it. You purchased that chair, or someone else did, so you could receive what it had to give: comfort, support, etc. But, when the time comes and that chair is no longer able to give what you need, what will you do with it? You'll get rid of it.

When a chair is no longer able to give us what we need, we find ourselves saying things like, "that chair is broken," or "that chair finally gave out," and we get rid of it. If someone else wants it, they'll have to fix it if they want to use it. Or, we'll put it out by the side of the street and the chair ultimately ends up at the dump where all the other useless, broken stuff goes. But did you know that even there, at the dump, that chair would still keep giving? Over the years, as it continues to break down, fall apart, decompose, and dissolve, it will keep giving back to the very ground from where it came. Know why? Because the principle of contagious generosity is built into every fiber of our universe, including chairs, and it never stops.

You'll die when you read this.

Let me illustrate it another way. Do you realize what happens when you die? If you're a Christian, you go to be with the Lord. The Bible says, "to be absent from the body is to be present with the Lord" (2 Corinthians 5:8). Your spirit goes to be with the Lord instantly. But what happens to your body? Did you realize it keeps giving? It will. Do you know why? Because the principle of contagious generosity is built into every aspect of our universe, including our bodies.

The principle of contagious generosity is built into every aspect of our universe, including our bodies.

Your body is the most phenomenal machine ever to grace this planet. Mankind is God's premier creation. Why? The reason is simple: man is created by God and in the image of God. Because of that, man has been able to create some incredible machines like laptops, cell phones, space shuttles, iPods, and HDTV. But nothing comes close to the human body. Why? Because even though God created man, man can't create like God.

That's why the uniqueness of the human eye can't be duplicated with high tech cameras, the human ear far eclipses man's best attempts at sound equipment, and the human hand, with its marvelous multiplicity of unmatched capabilities, can't be reproduced. Doctors and scientists have been able to develop prosthetic limbs, artificial hearts, hearing aids, even lasik surgery to improve our eyesight. But they've never been able to duplicate the unique, one-of-a-kind creation called the human body. It is God's personal, preeminent creation.

Like the rest of the universe, God built the principle of contagious generosity into every single cell of the human body. Every centimeter of skin, every artery, every muscle, every blood vessel and every organ is designed to give and to receive. You know what happens when they stop giving? We die.

God built the principle of contagious generosity into every single cell of the human body. Every centimeter of skin, every artery, every muscle, every blood vessel and every organ is designed to give and to receive.

Whether you realize it or not, we need our bodies to practice the principle of contagious generosity every day. In fact, our lives depend upon it. Keeping will kill us. If our bodies stop giving, generously, we're as good as dead.

Let's take it a step further. In a matter of a few hours after your death, you'll already be in the presence of the Lord, but most likely, your embalmed body will be in a casket somewhere. In a few more hours, after a bunch of nice people get together to sing some nice songs and say some nice things about you, they'll place that casket in the ground. A few hours later, someone will have covered your casket with dirt.

As time goes by, both your body and your casket will begin to decompose. Even though your body is dead, your body will still be giving, and so will your casket. That casket can only hold your body for so long, because it's giving, too. It's giving way to the earth above and around it. And, after a number of years, both your body and your casket will be one with the earth again. Our bodies and our caskets actually become dust again.

Genesis 2:7 says the Lord God "formed man from the dust of the ground and breathed into his nostrils the breath of life, and the man became a living being." In Psalm 90:3, the Psalmist says of God, "You turn men back to dust, saying, 'Return to dust, O sons of men.'" So, after we've been in the ground long enough, our bodies will keep giving until we are back to where we started. The giving process never stops. The

Unfortunately, some people will be better givers once they're dead.

principle of contagious generosity is built into every fiber of our universe and keeps on going . . . even after we die. Unfortunately, some people will be better givers once they're dead.

That leaves us with a critical question. If everything in the universe has been created to be generous, why are so many people selfish? Why are so many of us such prolific keepers, yet such poor givers? The simple answer is, we've missed God's best for our lives. Either we haven't been taught God's principles or we have been taught and we've chosen to ignore them.

God created every one of us to be generous. When we are generous, needs are met, lives are changed, the world becomes a better place, and God is honored and glorified. When we aren't generous, there are endless numbers of unmet needs and unchanged lives, and the world becomes a bitter place. Finally and tragically, God's purposes are delayed and God's glory is diminished when we aren't generous.

Do you have one of these in your garage?

As I was working on this book, I learned about one of the families in our church being generous. Apparently, they were having a garage sale. So they put up signs, advertised in the newspaper, and got all the items arranged just the way they wanted them. Finally the day arrived for the garage sale and people showed up. Carloads of people. As they began to mill around and look at all the items on display, they noticed something strange. Something completely different from all other garage sales. There were no price tags. A lady picked up an item and asked, "How much is this?" The homeowner (member of our church) said, "It's free." The lady was momentarily taken back and asked again, "It's free?" "Yes," the homeowner said. "It's all free."

You can probably imagine how fast the word spread and you know why? Generosity is always contagious! That morning, every single person who came to that garage sale was absolutely overwhelmed by the generosity of one of our church members who has obviously learned the principle of contagious generosity and is practicing it. T. Harv Eker said, "The mark of true wealth is determined by how much one can give away."

So am I encouraging you to start giving everything you have away? No, I'm just encouraging you to start giving and to start being generous—with your time, your talents, and the treasures God has given you. If you do, you can help change the world.

Proverbs 11:24-25 says, "One man gives freely, yet gains even more; another withholds unduly, but comes to poverty. A generous man will prosper; he who refreshes others will himself be refreshed." If you want to be blessed continuously, contagious generosity is the way to get there.

In the natural realm, you can't be contagious until you've caught the disease. In the supernatural realm, you're not contagious until you become generous. The good news is: we can all learn to be generous and live generous lives. When we do, we will find ourselves the recipients of God's ever-increasing, never-ending blessings.

. . . And, we'll become contagious!

Key Points to Remember:

- You and I weren't created to keep anything. We were created to give.

- God created everything in the universe to give and not to keep, and to be generous, not selfish.

- Nothing has a "shelf life." Everything is created to give. If it stays on the shelf, it becomes worthless.

- When we are generous, needs are met, lives are changed, the world becomes a better place, and God is honored and glorified.

- We can all learn to be generous and live generous lives.

"We make a living by what we get,
but we make a life by what we give."

—Winston Churchill

Now he who supplies seed to the sower
and bread for food will also supply
and increase your store of seed
and will enlarge the harvest of your righteousness.
You will be made rich in every way
so that you can be *generous* on every occasion,
and through us your *generosity*
will result in thanksgiving to God.
2 Corinthians 9:10-11

Chapter Two
Contagious Generosity
The Foundation of It

On the walls of the Baptist Temple church in Blue Bell, Pennsylvania, you'll find the picture of a little girl named Hattie May Wiatt. Her picture is precious. Her story is priceless. Her generosity, contagious!

In the early 1900s, Hattie May Wiatt was like most other elementary age children of her time. On Sundays, she went to Sunday school and church. Her pastor was Russell H. Conwell, the famous Baptist pastor and author of the best selling book, *Acres of Diamonds*. The building that housed the church was unfortunately small and very crowded. In fact, many times they would give out tickets for admission many weeks in advance for each of their services.

One particular Sunday, as Pastor Conwell walked up the street toward the church, he noticed a large number of children outside who were upset they couldn't get in due to the large number of children who were already in the Sunday school rooms. Some were trying to decide whether to stay or just go on back home. One of the little girls standing there was Hattie May Wiatt, books in hand along with her offering. Pastor Conwell took Hattie May in his arms, lifted her to his shoulder, and carried her inside the building to a Sunday school room, placing her in the only remaining seat in the corner.

The next day, as he was making his way to church, he walked by Hattie's house as she was on her way to school. He stopped and said, "Hattie, we are going to have a larger Sunday school room soon."

She replied, "I hope you will."

"Well," Pastor Conwell said, "when we get the money with which to erect a Sunday school building we are going to construct one large enough to get all the little children in, and we are going to begin very soon to raise the money for it."

At the time, Pastor Conwell later admitted, there really was no formal plan for such a building yet. It was just a vision in his mind. But he was trying to encourage Hattie and hoped she'd pass the word to others. The next day, he received word that Hattie had become very sick and the family asked him to come and pray for her. As he walked up the steps to her home, he prayed for her, but his heart ached knowing, somehow, she was not going to recover.

Later that week, Hattie May Wiatt died. After the funeral, her mother handed Pastor Conwell a little bag with 57¢ inside. Mrs. Wiatt explained that Hattie had wanted to give that money for the new Sunday school building at the church. On Sunday, he stood behind the pulpit announcing to the congregation that he had the first 57¢ towards the new Sunday school building. He offered the pennies for sale and received $250.00 for them. (Remember, this was the early

1900s.) Fifty-four of the original fifty-
seven pennies were returned to the pastor   *A little bag*
and he put them in a frame where they   *with 57¢ inside.*
could be on display.

With the $250.00 received for the original 57¢, the
church was able to purchase a house just north of their building. They tried to purchase an additional lot and when told
by the realtor it would cost $30,000, they said they only had
54¢ and asked for a mortgage on the rest. Obviously moved
and inspired by the story of Hattie May Wiatt's contribution,
the realtor accepted the framed 54¢ for the property and
eventually returned it to the church as a gift.

Within a period of less than five years, as her story was
shared again and again, Hattie's gift had grown to over a
quarter of a million dollars. The church grew to over 5600
members and her story inspired such generosity, they were
able to start Temple University and Temple University Hospital
(formerly Samaritan Hospital).

Over the years, because of little Hattie May Wiatt, millions of people have been inspired and moved to give millions of dollars to Christian causes.[1] Why? Because generosity is always contagious. Let me encourage you, like little
Hattie May Wiatt, to give to your local church and to the
Kingdom of God in such a way that when your story is told,
like Hattie's, it will honor the Lord and inspire the world.

He wrote the book on generosity.

Now, I want to show you the foundation of contagious
generosity. Where does it come from? It comes from God

The Bible opens and closes with the principle of contagious generosity. Himself and from His Word. The Bible opens and closes with the principle of contagious generosity. From the very first words of the opening book of the Bible, to the very last book, the Bible is the everlasting, ever-unfolding story of God's unlimited generosity.

Genesis 1:1 begins, "In the beginning God created the heavens and the earth." Talk about generosity. Look above and all around you. Everywhere you look, you'll see the most phenomenal demonstrations of God's generosity the world has ever seen. It's beyond description and beyond our ability to see it all, touch it all, understand it all, or even appreciate it all in our lifetime. The earth alone is an unfathomable expression of God's generosity. David said, "The earth is the LORD's and everything in it, the world and all who live in it" (Psalm 24:1). Isaiah said, "The whole earth is full of his glory" (Isaiah 6:3). The earth is one of many stupendous, prolific examples of the generosity of God. It bears His handprint, is blessed with His glory, and benefits His people.

Did you realize the Bible says that God, in His providential generosity, created the earth for us? Psalm 115:16 says, "The highest heavens belong to the LORD, but the earth he has given to man." And what a gift the earth was and is

God, in His providential generosity, created the earth for us. to man. It has everything we need to enjoy life—multitudes of resources, foods, minerals, vitamins, nutrients, materials to build with, materials to work with, materials to play with, you name it. And consider the fact that these resources have already been here for thousands of years and will be here long after you and I are gone.

If you take the time to read the first two chapters of Genesis, you will be overwhelmed at God's unequaled, indescribable generosity towards man. All of His magnificent creation was designed with you and me in mind. It's for us. Paul told Timothy, his young son in the faith, that God has given us everything we would ever need for our enjoyment (1 Timothy 6:17).

The ending's even better than the beginning.

Go to the final pages of your Bible and in the very last book, the book of Revelation, you'll find God, once again, demonstrating His unmatchable generosity by providing a place that was beyond John the Apostle's ability to describe. John talks about a place so incredible it's like a "bride beautifully dressed for her husband" (Revelation 21:2). It's a place where "everything is new" and "the old order of things has passed away" (Revelation 21:4-5). This place will surpass any place you and I have ever experienced in our entire lives. There won't be any more tears or tragedies, no more hurts, no more broken hearts, no more pain, no more suffering, and the best news of all: John says God is going to come and live with us (Revelation 21:3).

> *In Revelation, you'll find God, once again, demonstrating His unmatchable generosity by providing a place that was beyond John the Apostle's ability to describe.*

John says there is a great and high mountain and a

new city, the Holy City of Jerusalem (Revelation 21:10). He says it shines "with the glory of God, and its brilliance was like that of a very precious jewel" (Revelation 21:11). John also talks about a high wall with twelve gates, each made of a single pearl. He talks about the foundations of the city, decorated with every kind of precious stone you can possibly imagine. And yes, he talks about streets of gold (Revelation 21:21). But the best news of all? He says there is no need of a temple in the city because "the Lord God Almighty and the Lamb" are there (Revelation 21:22). It will be one of the most phenomenal demonstrations of God's generosity the world has ever seen.

The Bible begins and ends with the unparalleled, indescribable, unspeakable generosity of God.

So the Bible begins and ends with the unparalleled, indescribable, unspeakable generosity of God. Guess what's in the heart and soul of the Bible? Guess what you'll find right in the middle of God's Word? You'll find God's unfathomable, unequaled generosity. As a matter of fact, what you'll find there is the most phenomenal demonstration of God's generosity the world has ever known: the gift of His Son, the Lord, Jesus Christ.

Again, it's John the Apostle who's given the privilege of declaring the wondrous generosity of our Heavenly Father as He writes, "For God so loved the world that He gave His only begotten Son, that whosoever believeth on Him should not perish but have everlasting life" (John 3:16, KJV).

The very foundation of contagious generosity comes from God Himself and from His Word. His generosity is unmatched, and He calls each of us to be like Him. Paul told the Corinthian believers God is so committed to this concept of generosity, where each of us lives a lifestyle of continuous generosity, that He has committed Himself to help us do it. Second Corinthians 9:10-11 says, "Now he who supplies seed to the sower and bread for food will also supply and increase your store of seed and will enlarge the harvest of your righteousness. You will be made rich in every way so that you can be generous on every occasion, and through us your generosity will result in thanksgiving to God."

In other words, when we accept the assignment and make the commitment to be generous, God has promised to help us. In doing so, we will help meet the needs of God's people and provide a platform for many expressions of thanks to God (2 Corinthians 9:12). Paul goes on to say our example of living and giving generously will radically affect others and will encourage them to praise God because of His grace (2 Corinthians 9:13-14).

Generosity is not just important to God. It's imperative. God wants us to be generous. All of us—all the time. That's what He created us to do. He doesn't wink at our selfishness and give us the option of generosity, hoping we'll choose to be generous every now and then. Generosity needs to characterize our daily lives, especially when it comes to our relationship with God. Selfishness and stinginess won't be tolerated.

God wants us to be generous. All of us— all the time.

Guess what's happening tonight?

Jesus reinforced this when He told the parable of the rich fool. It's found in Luke 12:16-21. Read it again, carefully. "And he told them this parable: 'The ground of a certain rich man produced a good crop. He thought to himself, "What shall I do? I have no place to store my crops." 'Then he said, "This is what I'll do. I will tear down my barns and build bigger ones, and there I will store all my grain and my goods. And I'll say to myself, 'You have plenty of good things laid up for many years. Take life easy; eat drink and be merry.'" But God said to him, "You fool! This very night your life will be demanded from you. Then who will get what you have prepared for yourself?" **This is how it will be with anyone who stores up things for himself but is not rich toward God**'" (emphasis added).

Jesus emphatically declares our God-given responsibility to be generous when it comes to God. After all, our blessings come from God. James says, "every good and perfect gift is from above" (James 1:17). Moses warned God's people never to forget the Source of their blessings. He told them to "**remember the LORD your God, for it is he who gives you the ability to produce wealth**, and so confirms his covenant, which he swore to your forefathers, as it is today. **If you ever forget the LORD your God** and follow other gods and worship and bow down to them, I testify against you today that **you will surely be destroyed**. Like the nations the LORD destroyed before you, so you will be destroyed for not obeying the LORD your God" (Deut. 8:18-20, emphasis added).

God won't tolerate selfishness and stinginess. Remember: you and I weren't created to keep, we were created to give. To put it simply, selfishness and stinginess are ungodly. Un-God-like. (Let that sink in.) When we are self-centered and selfish, we aren't like God at all. We are utterly ungodly, and we'll pay a price for that.

Remember: you and I weren't created to keep, we were created to give.

Now I want to go back to the story of the rich fool Jesus talked about in Luke 12. If you look at the story carefully, this man was obviously blessed by God. The ground God had given Him produced a God-sized harvest. That's always the way it happens. Our harvest always comes from God, not from our own hands or our hard work.

Who's helping who here?

I heard the story years ago about a man who bought an old rundown farm. It had gone years without an owner and no real estate agent even wanted to list it. It was in severe disrepair, overgrown with weeds and brush. Fences were broken down and nearly gone. There were holes in the roof of the barn, windows broken in the farmhouse, and you couldn't even recognize the former harvest fields, which had produced so many years of bumper crops.

Eventually a man came along who purchased the old farm. He spent several months and several thousand dollars fixing up the place. One day, one of his friends came by to say hello. He got out of his truck, walked up to the farmer and said, "This place looks wonderful. You and God have really done a great job here." The farmer removed his hat and said, "You should have seen this place when God had it all to Himself."

God is the One Who brings the harvest, every time. You and I don't. Paul made this crystal clear in 1 Corinthians 3:6-7: "I planted the seed, Apollos watered it, but God made it grow. So neither he who plants nor he who waters is anything, but only God, who makes things grow." The devil doesn't either. The devil tries to take God's harvest away from you. Jesus said, "The thief (the devil) comes only to **steal** and **kill** and **destroy**." Jesus says, on the other hand, "I have come that you might have life and have it more abundantly" (John 10:10, paraphrased).

> *God is the One Who brings the harvest, every time.*

So the rich fool did what so many foolish people have done over the years: he started thinking the harvest was a result of his own efforts, and worse, that it belonged to him. Naturally, he had a problem. Since he thought it was the result of his work and was all reserved for him, obviously, he needed to have more storage units to contain it all. So, after giving it some thought, he decided to tear down the barns he had, to build bigger ones. That way he could store this huge harvest for himself and have it for many years to come. Then he decided he'd hold a party and celebrate his accomplishments.

The only problem was he didn't have just "a" problem. He had lots of problems. For one, the harvest came from Heaven, not in response to his hands or his hard work. Two, the harvest wasn't all about him. Nor was it all for him. It was God's blessing and for God's purposes. Sure, he could've used much of it to meet his needs. God always allows for, intends, and even encourages that. However, when God blesses us, He always has far more than just our needs in mind. He blesses us so we can bless Him and many others in the process.

Unfortunately, God was no longer in the picture for the rich fool. He was rich. But his swelling riches and recent success had crowded out the very Source of all his blessings. Tragically, even though he was buried beneath the blessings of God, he still thought it was all about him, his desires, and his dreams. Unfortunately, his dreams were about to become nightmares. Jesus acknowledged he was rich. But He also said he was a fool. Money doesn't make anyone wiser. In fact, money has been known to make people do some pretty dumb things. The rich fool is a classic illustration.

> *Money doesn't make anyone wiser. In fact, money has been known to make people do some pretty dumb things.*

"Money won't make you happy . . . but everybody wants to find out for themselves."

—Zig Ziglar

Be careful what you do with your blessings.

Over the years, I've met a lot of people similar to the "rich fool." These individuals were faithful and focused for God, at one time, while they were struggling to make ends meet. They never missed a worship service. You could tell they were in the Word on a regular basis. If the doors of the church were open, they were there—usually down front, serving with a smile, ready to do anything, involved in everything. Then success came. God answered their prayers and a harvest of God's blessings literally covered their lives. Maybe it was a job promotion or a deal that finally went through. In some cases it was a business that began to boom. Others received an unexpected amount of money from an inheritance, or a stock investment finally paid dividends. Regardless of the reason why things began to change for the better in their lives, regrettably, the results are often pathetically sad and predictably similar.

First, they begin to miss worship on the Lord's Day. Then, they are too busy to serve any more. Next thing you know, someone tells you they're not coming to church any more because someone offended them or something was done they didn't agree with or they have too much going on right now. The excuses come in all shapes and sizes. But the reality is always the same. Like the rich fool, they have become the recipients of God's harvest. Yet they have somehow completely forgotten God's generosity and submerged themselves in their own selfishness, bent on building bigger barns and partying on the profits for many years to come. Are they rich by the world's standards? Absolutely. But by God's standard, they are colossal fools.

In telling the parable of the rich fool, the point Jesus was making was that we have a God-given responsibility to be generous with God. After Jesus announced the tragic end of the rich fool: he was going to die and leave every bit of it behind and probably wouldn't even know who was going to get all of his stuff, including what barns he already had; Jesus said, "This is how it will be with anyone who stores up things for himself but is not rich toward God" (Luke 12:20).

Generosity is not optional for anyone or anything. It is foundational for everything in the universe God created. Even more so, generosity is essential for every child of God. When we give generously in response to His grace, the by-product of our generosity will be God's hand of blessing upon us.

Halfhearted generosity won't cut it either. In fact, that's really an oxymoron, isn't it? "Halfhearted generosity"? That would be like a "halfhearted follower of Jesus Christ." It just doesn't work. Like half-hearted obedience or half-hearted commitment, any-thing less than wholehearted generosity will not and cannot please or honor God.

> *Like halfhearted obedience or halfhearted commitment, anything less than whole-hearted generosity will not and cannot please or honor God.*

Something's better than nothing, isn't it?

The people of Israel found out what God thinks of half-hearted generosity. In Malachi 1:8, God rebuked the priests of Israel for bringing blind, crippled, and diseased animals for the sacrifices which were supposed to be for the worship of God. Where do you think the good animals were? Want to guess where they'd put the animals without spot or blemish? Obviously, they weren't offering them to God. You think they might have been keeping them for themselves? Good guess.

God then rebukes the priests of Israel and says, "Try offering these diseased, blind, and crippled animals to your governor and watch what happens. Do you think he'll be happy and accept you?" (Malachi 1:8, paraphrased). The obvious answer was: "Of course not!"

Now I'm not sure God intended this to be humorous. But what He says here is actually quite humorous (at least from my perspective). God is actually saying, "Try offering these blind, crippled, diseased animals to a politician— someone who makes his living compromising and cutting corners. You think he'll take them from you? Not a chance!"

Then God makes a startling statement, **"'Oh, that one of you would shut the temple doors, so that you would not light useless fires on my altar! I am not pleased with you,' says the LORD Almighty, 'and I will accept no offerings from your hands.** My name will be great among the nations, from the rising to the setting of the sun. In every place incense and pure offerings will be brought to my name, because my name will be great among the nations'" (Malachi 1:10-11, emphasis added).

Now get the picture. Here were the priests of Israel giving to God, which is exactly what they were supposed to be doing. However, they weren't giving their best. They were giving, but like many people still do today, they kept the best for themselves and gave God leftovers. In actuality, they were giving God rejects, animals that no one else wanted: blind,

Like many people still do today, they kept the best for themselves and gave God leftovers.

diseased, and crippled animals. Can you imagine someone doing that? And God tells them, "I wish you'd just shut the doors of the temple! You are wasting your time and Mine. I will not receive such offerings from your hands."

Does God have a word for us today?

I wonder what God would say to the average church in America today? If you check the giving habits of contemporary, evangelical Christians in America, you will discover a large portion of the leaders and people in those churches don't even tithe. Wonder what God would say to the masses of contemporary church members who keep the best for themselves and give Him their leftovers? I think we have a pretty good idea, don't you?

Far too often, we attempt to excuse ourselves from what God expects, and yet somehow still expect His blessing. It won't work. That's why Jesus shared the parable of the rich fool in Luke 12.

In **Proverbs 3:9-10**, Solomon, one of the wisest men who ever lived, shares some incredible wisdom. He says, "Honor the LORD with your wealth, with the **firstfruits** of all your crops; then your barns will be filled to overflowing, and your vats will brim over with new wine" (emphasis added). Solomon says we need to be generous first and foremost with the Giver of every blessing we receive: God. Whatever wealth we receive, whatever blessings we become the beneficiaries of, we need to recognize it all comes from

Whatever wealth we receive, we need to recognize it all comes from God and make sure we give back to Him.

God and make sure we give back to Him from the very first-fruits of those blessings. Everything we have and everything we receive comes from and belongs to God (James 1:17, Psalm 24:1).

To put it simply, the first check we write every week when we get paid should be the check we write to God. Before anything or anyone else, God should be first. He deserves our best, our firstfruits. Whenever we receive a blessing, expected (like our regular salary) or unexpected (like a bonus, raise or gift of some kind), we need to make sure the first thing we do is recognize, thank, and bless God. How can we do that? By giving the firstfruits, the first check, to God through our local church (see Malachi 3:10).

We're not going to miss out on anything by being generous with God. Quite the contrary, our choosing to be generous is what ensures God's hand of blessing will be on us, meeting all of our needs and then some (Philippians 4:19). You absolutely, positively cannot *out-give* God! Solomon says, "One man gives freely (generously), yet gains even more; another withholds unduly (acts selfishly), but comes to poverty" (Proverbs 11:24). Generosity will bring additional blessings, while selfishness stops God's blessings from coming our way.

We don't give to get, but guess what you get when you give?

Solomon said, "A generous man will prosper; he who refreshes others will himself be refreshed" (Proverbs 11:25). Now, our motivation for being generous is not so our needs will be met. However, it is an unalterable promise of Scripture that when we meet the needs of others by being generous, God will be generous with us and will meet our needs. When we dedicate our lives to refreshing the lives of others, God will bless and refresh us.

Paul told the Corinthians, "Remember this: Whoever sows sparingly will also reap sparingly, and whoever sows generously will also reap generously" (2 Corinthians 9:6). We don't lose a thing by being generous. It's when we refuse to be generous that we lose.

> *When we dedicate our lives to refreshing the lives of others, God will bless and refresh us.*

So, the foundation for contagious generosity is God and His Word. God wants every one of us to be generous, because when we are, we are most like Him. When we are selfish, we are most like the devil. So the choice is ours when it comes to who we want to be like: God or the devil. The choice to be generous, however, is not ours. God made that choice for us before the creation of the world. He wants you and me to be generous. That's the way He created us. We weren't created to keep anything. We were created to give — everything. By being generous, not only are we like Him and doing what He created us to do, but we also have the benefit of experiencing His continuous blessings in our lives.

Being generous is absolutely foundational to everything we want to do in life, if we want to do it the way we're supposed to — God's way.

Key Points to Remember:

- The Bible is the everlasting, ever-unfolding story of God's generosity.

- Generosity is not just important to God, it's imperative.

- When we are self-centered and selfish, we aren't like God at all.

- Anything less than wholehearted generosity will not and cannot please or honor God.

- We're not going to miss out on anything in life by being generous with God. Quite the contrary, our choosing to be generous is what ensures God's hand of blessing will be on us.

"God's work done in God's way will never lack God's supply."

—Hudson Taylor

Command those who are rich in this present world
not to be arrogant nor to put their hope in wealth,
which is so uncertain, but to put their hope in God,
who richly provides us with everything for our enjoyment.
Command them to do good, to be rich in good deeds,
and to be *generous* and willing to share.
In this way they will lay up treasure for themselves
as a firm foundation for the coming age,
so that they may take hold of the life that is truly life.
1 Timothy 6:17-19

CHAPTER THREE

Contagious Generosity
THE ILLUSTRATION OF IT

You'll always recognize contagious generosity. Sometimes it even shows up at work. Now most people would probably never refer to their boss using the words "good as gold." However, every single employee of the Thompson-McCully Company would. Why? To understand, we have to go back to the beginning.

Bob Thompson, from Belleville, Michigan, lived in the same modest house the majority of his adult life. He started a business in his basement, supported by his wife who was a school teacher. Over a forty-year period, he expanded the asphalt company he owned into a phenomenal road-building enterprise.

If you were to visit his office, you wouldn't find the trappings that normally characterize a CEO's office: Persian rugs, expensive antiques, oil paintings, etc. Instead, what you would find are pictures of his three children and five grandchildren. You'd also find a number of Norman Rockwell prints, a copy of John Donne's "No Man Is An Island" meditation, and a clock with its hands frozen at almost 3 o'clock. Mr. Thompson didn't play the stock market, own a private jet, or ride around on a luxury yacht. He didn't belong to a country club or collect the toys of his rich contemporaries. He did drive a Lincoln, and occasionally, he and his wife would take in a Broadway show.

He sold his company to CRH, a building and construction firm based in Dublin, Ireland. He chose this company because of their record of unifying companies and maintaining workers and even agreed to stay on and run the business. CRH paid him $422 million dollars.

So, what did he do with all that money? For years he had shared a secret plan with his wife. He'd always planned to reward his workers and had named scores of them in his will. But no one had any idea how big a reward they were about to receive. The announcement was made by sending a letter to all of his workers. It began assuring them no one would lose their jobs. It ended telling them they would each share in the proceeds of the sale.

Bob and his wife divided up $128 million dollars among his 550 workers and gave an unbelievable bonus to more than 80 of them: they would become instant millionaires. He even paid the taxes for them, which came to $25 million, purposely ensuring that "workers given $1 million each would reach that magical milestone," he said.

The checks were distributed on a Sunday morning in the seven Thompson-McCully offices all over Michigan. Instantly, it was as if dozens of workers had won the lottery. There were lots of tears and hugs. Many were left speechless. Hourly workers, most of whom had pensions or 401k plans, received $2,000 for each year of service to the company;

some checks exceeded annual salaries. Salaried workers, who had no pensions, were given checks or annuity certificates they could cash in when they reached age 55 or 62. Those ranged from $1 million to $2 million each.

Mr. Thompson even included retirees and widows in his generous plan. He also said he and his wife planned to give away most of what was left of the $422 million.

Many of the workers were so emotional they couldn't talk without crying. So Mr. Thompson told them just to write a note and within a couple of weeks, his mailbox was full with over 550 letters of thanks. "It's the stuff children's fairy tales are made of," wrote a worker's wife, one of many who wrote on their husbands' behalf. "What do I say to you for changing our lives and handing us a future we have never dreamed of?" Some of the workers said they were instantly inspired to help others. Genuine generosity is always contagious.[1]

I'm challenging you to start trying to live, love, give, and work as generously as you possibly can.

I'm challenging you to start trying to live, love, give, and work as generously as you possibly can. Whether you own your own company or you're an employee working for someone else, you're not going to lose a thing because you're generous. In fact, you're going to discover genuine generosity has a boomerang effect and you'll actually receive more than you give.

Generous obedience always results in generous blessing.

There are all kinds of illustrations of generosity like Bob Thompson and the Thompson-McCully Company. One of the best is the story of Pastor Rick Warren. Rick and his wife founded Saddleback Community Church in Lake Forest, California, in 1980 with one family. Today their church averages close to 25,000 on a 125-acre campus. Rick has become one of the most influential Christian leaders in our world. His book, *The Purpose Driven Life*, sold over 40 million books and instantly made him a very wealthy man. What he and his wife Kay did next is an incredible example of contagious generosity. They decided they wouldn't alter their lifestyle one bit and didn't make any major purchases. Then Rick decided to stop taking a salary from Saddleback. In fact, he added up what the church had paid him in the 24 years he had served there and wrote a check to pay it all back. Next, he and his wife set up three foundations to fund an initiative they call *The Peace Plan*, which helps people infected by AIDS, trains church leaders in developing countries, and helps fight poverty, disease, and illiteracy around the globe. Oh, one more thing, Rick and Kay now live on 10% and give 90% of their income away. Their story is another powerful testimony that you don't lose anything by being generous.

Since the beginning of time, there have been multitudes of people who have taken God at His Word and have decided to live a life of contagious generosity.

Since the beginning of time, there have been multitudes of people who have taken God at His Word and have decided to live a life of contagious generosity. Some of the most inspiring stories come from the Bible. Others come from people whose lives have been changed by the Bible. Hopefully, the illustrations you're about to read will help challenge you to become a person of contagious generosity so your life can change others the way their stories are about to change you!

In Genesis 12, God told Abram (Abraham) He wanted him to leave his home and travel to a place God would show him. God didn't tell Abram why, but He did tell him, "I will make you into a great nation and I will bless you; I will make your name great, and you will be a blessing. I will bless those who bless you and whoever curses you I will curse; and all peoples on earth will be blessed by you" (Genesis 12:2-3).

All of that sounds wonderful. But remember, Abram had to leave home for any of that to happen. What would it take for you to be willing to leave your home, your family, and friends? I thought so. Most of us would say, "Not so fast, God. I want a chance to think about this." Some of us would probably even attempt to negotiate with God. However, the very next verse says, "So Abram left, as the LORD had told him" (Genesis 12:4). That verse also tells us Abram was seventy-five years old when he left home.

So we're talking about a major, abrupt, drastic, radical change for Abram. It would be for anyone, especially if you were already 75 years of age. Just think about uprooting your family and leaving everything familiar behind. That's what Abram did. But his generous obedience didn't stop there.

Abram even began to practice God's generosity with others. His nephew, Lot, had accompanied him on the same trip from their homeland in Haran. Lot had a number of herds and herdsmen who began to quarrel with those who belonged to Abram. To settle the dispute, Abram told his nephew to choose for himself where he wanted to go, and whatever direction he chose, Abram promised he would go the other way. Talk about a generous offer. Lot selected what appeared to be the best land available. But once again, God rewarded Abram, and after Lot and his entourage had left for the well-watered plains of the Jordan, God called Abram aside and said, "Lift up your eyes from where you are and look north and south, east and west. All the land that you see I will give to you and your offspring forever" (Genesis 13:14-15).

Don't miss this: Abram's generous obedience and abundant generosity resulted in even greater blessings for him and his family. And God wasn't finished. In Genesis 17, God changed Abram's name to Abraham and promised he would be the "father of many nations." However, in Genesis 22, God tested Abraham again. He asked Abraham to offer his son as a sacrifice. You know what's worse than having to leave your home to go to a strange place you know nothing about? How about giving up a child?

Once again though, Abraham responded in faith, obeyed God, and was rewarded for his obedience with another promise of God's generous blessing. God said, "I will surely bless you and make your descendants as numerous as the stars in the sky and as

Generous obedience will always bring God's generous blessing.

the sand on the seashore. Your descendants will take possession of the cities of their enemies and through your offspring, all nations on earth will blessed, because you have obeyed me" (Genesis 22:17-18). Generous obedience will always bring God's generous blessing.

Maybe it's not the last supper.

Another terrific illustration of generosity is found in 1 Kings 17, where we are introduced to the widow at Zarephath. The Bible tells us there had been no rain in the land, and God had told Elijah to go to Zarephath of Sidon and stay there. So Elijah went and when he arrived, he came upon a widow who was gathering sticks. He asked her for a drink of water. As she was leaving to get him a drink, Elijah also asked for a piece of bread. The widow responded, "As surely as the LORD your God lives, I don't have any bread— only a handful of flour in a jar and a little oil in a jug. I am gathering a few sticks to take home and make a meal for myself and my son, that we may eat it—and die" (1 Kings 17:12).

Talk about an impossible situation. Because of the lack of rain food was scarce, and these were tough times for everyone. But even more so for this widow because she was on her own and no doubt had a hard time providing for herself and her son. In the midst of her crisis, Elijah instructs her to go home and make a small cake of bread for him from what she had. Imagine that! Then, he told her to make something for herself and her son. His next statement is powerful. He said, "For this is what the LORD, the God of Israel says: 'The jar of flour will not be used up and the jug of oil will not run dry until the day the LORD gives rain on the land'" (1 Kings 17:14).

Elijah was telling her, if she would be generous with what she had, God was going to be so generous with her that she wouldn't run out of flour or oil. She could make all kinds of cakes and bake all kinds of bread until the day God would send rain on the land. That meant she would be provided for generously, until God provided another source of generous provisions for her and her son.

The Bible says the widow went and did exactly as Elijah had instructed her, and there was more than enough food every day for Elijah, the widow, and her son (1 Kings 17:15-16).

When you and I are generous, God will always be generous with us, and He's not going to run out of resources to provide for us. The widow at Zarephath had to take a serious step of faith in light of her circumstances. She only had enough flour and oil for one last supper to do what Elijah told her to do. But, she stepped out in faith and gave generously. The result was that she received far more than she gave, the needs of others were met, and her needs were met as well.

When we step out in faith to be generous, God will always step in to provide for our needs.

When we step out in faith to be generous, God will always step in to provide for our needs. He will do it in such a generous fashion, it will absolutely eclipse what we could have done had we attempted to meet our own needs.

A jarring example.

In 2 Kings 4, we're introduced to another widow. This time, it's a preacher's wife whose husband died and left her alone with two sons. She'd exhausted every last resource and was on the verge of losing everything, including her two sons to a creditor who wanted to make them his slaves. In absolute desperation, she cried out to the prophet Elisha for help. Like Elijah before him, he asked the widow what she had in her house. Her reply was that all they had left was a little oil (2 Kings 4:2). Elisha then told her to go and ask her neighbors for empty jars. Now there's a strange request for you. This request is quite similar to what God told Abram to do when He was told to pack up and leave home at the age of seventy-five. Nevertheless, the widow went and asked for jars. Elisha told her to take what oil she had left and pour it into those jars.

That poor widow had to give what she had in order to receive what God had. It always works that way. I can't count the number of times I've heard people say, "But I can't afford to give." Truth is, we can't afford **not** to give. Giving is how we connect with God's blessing. If you keep what you have, God will keep what He has. Keeping cuts us off from His blessing, whereas giving brings us under His blessings. Remember: God didn't create us to be keepers. He created us to be givers. That's why Jesus said, "Give and it shall be given to you" (Luke 6:38). The reverse of that is also true: keep and it shall be kept from you.

Remember: God didn't create us to be keepers. He created us to be givers.

The Bible says the widow began filling jars, and when she had filled the final jar, the oil stopped flowing. Amazingly, she was able to sell the extra oil she now had (thanks to God's generous provision), and pay all of her remaining debts. I've often wondered if she got every possible jar she could have from her neighbors. Or, once the miracle of God's provision started filling those vessels to the top, did she say to her two sons, "I wish we had more jars"?

We can learn a lot from the widow of 2 Kings 4. For example, we need to realize our problems are merely platforms for God's provision. He allows us to have needs so we will turn to Him for His provision. If we don't turn to Him, our needs will never be fully met and He will keep sending needs our way until He gets our attention and our obedience.

Our problems are merely platforms for God's provision.

Here's another lesson for us to learn: Don't miss God's blessings by keeping instead of giving what you have, even when you think what you have isn't much. When we keep instead of give, we always miss the blessing. Here's one more: Don't limit God's blessing by a lack of faith or an unwillingness to do whatever God tells you to do. Remember, generous obedience will always result in God's generous blessing. And His blessing will come in a variety of ways, not just financial or material.

Genuine love is always generous.

One of the most remarkable illustrations of generosity comes from the New Testament. Jesus had returned to Bethany, the home of his close friends, Mary, Martha, and Lazarus. A dinner was being held in the home of Simon the Leper to honor Jesus (Matthew 26:6). Everyone was sharing his or her love and gratitude to Jesus. Among them was Lazarus, who had recently been raised from the dead by the

Lord, and Simon, whom the Lord had healed of leprosy. It must've been an incredible night of praise and worship as they showed their gratitude and love for Jesus. In the midst of all that, Mary gets up and takes an extremely expensive bottle of perfume, worth three hundred days' wages, and pours it all over Jesus. It was a spontaneous act of generosity, which ended with her wiping the Lord's feet with her own hair.

Judas immediately objected and put his mouth where his wicked heart was. He said, "Why wasn't this perfume sold and the money given to the poor? It was worth a year's wages" (John 12:5). His comment gave the appearance of some degree of spirituality and even concern for others. John, however, gives another perspective. John says Judas "did not say this because he cared for the poor but because he was a thief; as keeper of the money bag, he used to help himself to what was put into it" (John 12:6).

Jesus responded, "Leave her alone" (John 12:7). "I tell you the truth, wherever this gospel is preached throughout the world, what she has done will also be told in memory of her" (Matthew 26:13). Jesus appreciated and affirmed her generosity and declared that her story would be told for generations to come. He went on to say that wherever her story is told, people would honor her and what she had done forever. Why? Generosity is always contagious.

What Mary did, giving the best she had, in a spontaneous act of extravagant love and worship of Jesus, is a tremendous example of contagious generosity. Her story also reminds us we can never overdo it when it comes to

We can never overdo it when it comes to giving our best to Jesus.

giving our best to Jesus. Maybe we should try to do that more often.

We don't need fast food. We just need food—fast.

Another excellent example of contagious generosity is the feeding of the 5,000 in the Gospel of John. Remember the story of the boy with five loaves of bread and two small fish? Huge crowds had been following Jesus because of the miraculous signs He had been performing. On one particular day, Jesus saw a huge crowd coming and asked Philip, "Where shall we buy bread for these people to eat?" (John 6:5). Phillip's response was that "eight months' wages would not buy enough bread for each one to have a bite!" (John 6:7).

About the same time, Andrew showed up with a boy who had five small barley loaves and two small fish. The implication is clear that this young boy offered to share what he had to help meet the need. (The disciples would never have taken the bread and fish from him had he not offered them willingly.) But even with this act of generosity on the part of a young boy, the disciples were still perplexed as to how this could possibly help the present dilemma.

Jesus tells the disciples to have the people sit down, and He then prayed over the bread and fish (John 6:10). The Holy Spirit also notes there were at least five thousand men present. Which means there were most likely several thousand women and children as well.

What happens next is . . . well, miraculous. When Jesus finished praying, the disciples started distributing bread and fish to every person in this crowd of thousands. John says when everyone had been fed, the Lord told the disciples to gather up what was left over, and there were twelve full baskets with bread still in them. Remarkable? Yes. Unusual? No. All Jesus did was respond to the generosity of one young boy, met the needs of thousands of people in the process, and was so generous in His blessings, there were leftovers.

That's the way our generous God always operates. He always gives more than enough, more than we expect, more than we need, and more than we can possibly use for ourselves, so we can be generous with others.

God is just waiting to see our generosity so He can show us His, and He will never be surpassed by anyone.

Generosity is always overwhelming. It's also contagious. What's more, God is just waiting to see our generosity so He can show us His, and He will never be surpassed by anyone.

No small conversion.

Another wonderful example of generosity comes from the gospel of Luke. It's the story of Zacchaeus, the tax collector. You may remember singing that little song about Zacchaeus when you were growing up. The "wee little man" who "climbed up in the sycamore tree" so he could see Jesus. Remember? Well, even though Zacchaeus was small in stature, what he ended up doing was no small thing.

That day, Zacchaeus not only saw Jesus, but even had the Lord as a guest in his home. Can you imagine that? He even got saved. How do we know? Because the Lord said so, in Luke 19:9, "Today salvation has come to this house."

Luke tells us salvation had an immediate impact upon Zacchaeus, too. In Luke 19:8, the Bible says, "Zacchaeus stood up and said to the Lord, 'Look, Lord! Here and now I give half of my possessions to the poor, and if I have cheated anybody out of anything, I will pay back four times the amount.'"

Did you catch that? Luke tells us Zacchaeus's salvation resulted in immediate generosity. Genuine salvation always does. That's why every time someone is saved, not only does the Kingdom grow but the resources of the Kingdom should grow as well. Unfortunately it doesn't always happen that way because some people erroneously believe salvation does not include our checkbook, pocketbook, wallet, or bank account. However, the story of Zacchaeus graphically illustrates that it does.

One of the very first indications of our salvation should be a spirit of generosity and giving that mirrors the spirit of generosity and giving of the One Who saved us. The Bible says, "Therefore, if anyone is in Christ, he is a new creation; old things have passed away; behold, all things have become new" (2 Corinthians 5:17, KJV). Wouldn't you think our salvation would provide us with a new spirit of generosity and giving to replace our old selfishness and stinginess? Regardless of what you and I may think, that's exactly what genuine salvation does.

For years, stewardship and giving consultants have told us it takes three years to develop a tither, someone who gives 10% of his income back to God. (See Malachi 3:10.) However, the testimony of Zacchaeus teaches the exact opposite. It shouldn't take three years for someone to get to the place where he is regularly and faithfully generous in his giving to God and His church every week. What's more, the church shouldn't allow that to keep happening over and over. We wouldn't consider someone saved who didn't read the Bible, pray, or come to church for three years. So why would we look the other way when someone's giving isn't even close to the biblical tithe, giving ten percent? Maybe, like in the story of Zacchaeus, Jesus needs to make more house calls.

> *It shouldn't take three years for someone to get to the place where he is regularly and faithfully generous in his giving to God and His church every week.*

I heard the story of two brothers who worked on a family farm their father had left in his will. One brother was married and had a family. The other brother had remained single. At the end of every day, the brothers would divide equally the produce and profit from the farm.

One day, the brother who was single said to himself, "My brother and I shouldn't be dividing the produce and profit from dad's farm right down the middle. After all he has a family and I'm single. I don't need as much as he does." So, he began to take a sack of grain from his storage bin each night and went over to his brother's bin and dumped it in.

Meanwhile, the brother who was married said to himself, "My brother and I shouldn't be dividing the produce and profit from Dad's farm right down the middle. After all, I'm married and I have a wonderful family. My brother has no one to share his life with or to care for him in the years to come." So, he began to take a sack of grain from his storage bin each night and went over to his brother's bin and dumped it in.

For years, both brothers were puzzled by the fact that their supply of grain never diminished. Then one night, it was dark and a fog had set in over the family farm. Both brothers got the sack of grain, as they always had done, and began to take it to the other brother's storage bin, when they accidentally bumped into each other. Instantly it dawned on them what had been happening all those years. They dropped their sacks, embraced, and wept over each other's act of generosity.

When someone tells your story, will it be a story of contagious generosity? It should be and it can be. But only you can make sure it will be.

Key Points to Remember:

- Genuine generosity has a boomerang effect and you'll actually receive more than you give.

- Generous obedience will always be met with God's generous blessing.

- When we step out in faith to be generous, God will always step in to provide for our needs.

- We can never overdo it when it comes to giving our best to Jesus.

- God is just waiting to see our generosity so He can show us His, and He will never be surpassed by anyone.

"You have not lived today until
you have done something
for someone who can never repay you."
—John Bunyan

"Honor the LORD with your wealth,
with the *firstfruits* of all your crops;
then your barns will be filled to overflowing,
and your vats will brim over with new wine."
Proverbs 3:9-10

CHAPTER FOUR
Contagious Generosity
THE DEMONSTRATION OF IT

One of the largest single donations ever given to a charitable organization was given in 2004. It was a gift in excess of $1.5 billion dollars and was given to a church organization: the Salvation Army. Famous for its red Christmas kettles and tireless bell ringers, the Salvation Army was the recipient of a gift from an organization famous for its golden arches: McDonald's.

Burger king is generous because of McDonald's.

The gift came from the estate of Mrs. Joan Kroc, wife of hamburger tycoon, Ray Kroc. Joan died in October of 2003. The Salvation Army, which promises "soup, soap, and salvation" was a favorite of her husband who died in 1984. Mr. Kroc had actually served as a "bell ringer" for the organization in the 1950s and '60s. Half of the gift, at Mrs. Kroc's request, was placed in an endowment from which the earnings will be used as income to help support operation of the centers. The other half will cover the cost of building them. Mrs. Kroc also made a previous donation to the Salvation

Army in 1998 worth $92 million to help underwrite the Ray and Joan Kroc Corps Community Center in San Diego. Talk about super-sized stewardship!

While a gift of $1.5 billion is certainly unique and probably well beyond the reach of most of the readers of this book, the truth is, every single one of us can become generous Christian philanthropists and super-size our impact for the Kingdom of God.[1]

How? Step one is to become a faithful tither (giving 10% of your income) to your local church every week. If you've already made that commitment—way to go! You're already on your way. If you haven't made the commitment to be a tither yet, you still have a ways to go if you want to practice contagious generosity.

When every Christian tithes, the size and impact of such giving can be absolutely enormous for every local church and for the Kingdom of God at large. The blessings for every tither will be absolutely enormous as well (see Malachi 3:10). When Christians give generous love offerings above and beyond the tithe, the blessings compound exponentially both for them and their church and the ministries and missions their church supports.

> *When every Christian tithes, the size and impact of such giving can be absolutely enormous for every local church and for the Kingdom of God at large.*

In the October 2005 issue of *World Magazine*, Cultural Editor Gene Edward Veith, wrote, "If church members were to tithe 10 percent of their income, churches would reap an additional $156 billion. And, according to calculations in the study, if 60 percent of that extra income were designated for overseas missions, that would come to $94 billion—enough to feed, medicate and evangelize the underdeveloped world."[2] Can you imagine churches having **an additional $156 billion**? God can. That's why He instituted the tithe.

The second step to becoming a generous, Christian philanthropist is to make generosity a way of life. As we've already seen, God has a way of making sure generous people can always be generous on every occasion (2 Corinthians 9:10-11). Selfish people never have enough. Generous people always have more than enough. Know why that is? Again, Proverbs 11:24-25 says, "One man gives freely, yet gains even more; another withholds unduly, but comes to poverty. A generous man will prosper; he who refreshes others will himself be refreshed." God created all of us to be generous, and when we are, He steps in to help us so we can continue to be generous.

If you are already a tither, why not make the decision right now, if you haven't already, to incorporate generosity into your lifestyle and the lifestyle of your family and business by giving above and beyond the tithe every week for the rest of your life? You absolutely cannot lose because God promises to bless those who are generous with His continuous blessings.

The third step to becoming a generous Christian philanthropist and making a huge impact on our world is to make all you can, invest all you can, and save all you can so you can give all you can. One of the greatest financial discover-

ies anyone ever makes is that we are going to leave everything behind. Everything! Whatever wealth we have is only
ours temporarily and will ultimately return to its Rightful
Owner: God. Since it's not ours and it's not primarily for us,
logic would tell us it must be
for something else. Here is
that something else: Whatever wealth we have is a gift
from God and He expects
us to give **passionately**
(2 Corinthians 9:6-7), **pur-
posefully** (Matthew 6:19-21) and **proportionately** (Luke
12:48) so He can use it to build His Kingdom.

*Whatever wealth we have is
only ours temporarily and
will ultimately return
to its Rightful Owner: God.*

Next time you visit a McDonald's for lunch, don't super-
size your meal. Instead, remember the example of Ray and
Joan Kroc, and recommit yourself to live and give generously in such a way you can super-size your impact for the
Kingdom of God.

As we have already seen, God created us to be givers,
not keepers. And He created us to be generous givers, too.
God has called every one of us to demonstrate a lifestyle of
generosity to the selfish, self-serving, self-centered society in
which we find ourselves. He wants us to be generous and to
live lives of generosity because that goes against the grain of
everything in our culture. It flies in the face of a world looking out for #1, and causes people to sit up and take notice.
In other words, it's contagious. Why? Because generosity is
so "other-worldly."

Besides being contagious, our generosity actually provides a platform for us to present Christ to a watching, won-

dering, bewildered world that knows instinctively selfishness is not the way to genuine, life-long, life-fulfilling success (Romans 1:18-20).

God has called every one of us to demonstrate a lifestyle of generosity to the selfish, self-serving, self-centered society in which we find ourselves.

So how can we demonstrate contagious generosity?

Even though in Christ we are under grace and no longer bound by the Old Testament law, the measuring stick of "generosity" *begins* with the Old Testament tithe. Let me share with you why I believe every Christian should, at the bare minimum, tithe, and why that level is the starting point for contagious generosity.

First of all, we need to understand the difference between obedience and generosity. Those are two totally different things. Until we've been obedient to God, we can't call anything we give generosity. To understand the difference we need to go back to Malachi 3 where God clearly differentiates between tithes (obedience) and offerings (generosity).

Tithing is not an act of generosity. Rather, it is an act of obedience.

In Malachi 3:8-10, God rebukes the people of Israel for robbing Him and says they have robbed Him "in tithes and offerings." From God's perspective, tithes and offerings are two completely different things. The tithe is giving 10% of one's income back to Him through your local church. Tithing is not an offering and an offering is not a tithe. God says they are two completely different things.

You can't put $5 in an offering and call it a "tithe" unless your total income for that week was only $50. You also can't call that $5 an offering until you've tithed (given God 10% of your weekly income). Why not? We can't honor and please God until we've obeyed God. Tithing, giving 10% of our income back to God, is obedience. The firstfruits of all of our increase (income) belong to God (Proverbs 3:9-10).

When I was growing up, I remember hearing churches use the slogan: "we pay our tithe, we give our offerings." We don't hear that much anymore. But theologically, those eight words hit the bull's eye. The tithe is what rightfully belongs to God, 10% of whatever He blesses us with each week. Because it belongs to God, we really do "pay" the tithe. It is an act of obedience. Once we have given the tithe, we are free to give an offering, as we are led by the Spirit, to our church or any other ministry we choose to support. It is my conviction, from a biblical and practical standpoint, we can't call anything we give to God an "offering" until we have tithed (given 10% of our income) to Him through the local church.

Isn't tithing just an Old Testament doctrine?

No. Tithing isn't just an Old Testament doctrine, even though you'll find it there. It's a Bible doctrine, because you not only find it in the Old Testament, but in the New Testament as well. This comes as a surprise to many people, especially those who don't tithe and use it as an excuse.

In **Matthew 23:23**, Jesus rebukes the teachers of the law and the Pharisees when He says, "Woe to you, teachers of the law and Pharisees, you hypocrites! You give a **tenth** (a tithe) of your spices—mint, dill and cummin. But you have neglected the more important matters of the law—justice, mercy and faithfulness. *You should have practiced the latter, without neglecting the former.*" Now, if tithing were just an Old Testament doctrine and had no place in the New Testament economy, this would have been an ideal place for Jesus to say, "Hey, fellas. What are you doing tithing? You don't need to do that any more. Tithing was an Old Testament doctrine and you are no longer under any obligation to give my Father ten percent of your income."

But that's not what Jesus said. Here were these legalistic Pharisees, faithfully and fastidiously tithing everything down to the most minute spices you could possess. (Yes, they were legalistic. But you have to admire their obedience in tithing.) Jesus rebuked them, not for being such meticulous tithers, but for ignoring the more important matters of the law such as justice, mercy, and faithfulness. Don't miss this: He did **not** rebuke their obedience in tithing those three tiny spices. Rather, He encouraged them, in addition to their obedience in tithing, to make sure they didn't neglect justice, mercy, and faithfulness.

Luke 11:42 also addresses the subject of tithing. Here again are the words of Jesus, "Woe to you Pharisees, because you give God a **tenth** of your mint, rue and all other kinds of garden herbs, but you neglect justice and the love of God. You should have practiced the latter without leaving the former undone." Again, if tithing were no longer a part of God's plan—relegated only to Old Testament times and Old Testament saints—this would have been the perfect place for Jesus to set the record straight. However, Jesus does the exact opposite. He says, *"you should have practiced the latter without leaving the former undone."*

Tithing is also mentioned in **Luke 18:12**. Here, Jesus is telling a parable to illustrate the folly of self-righteousness. He mentions a Pharisee who stood up and bragged that he was not like a tax collector, saying, "I fast twice a week and give a tenth of all I get." Now if tithing was only for Old Testament Israelites and had no bearing or importance to anyone living during New Testament times or beyond, why would Jesus use it in an illustration when He's trying to communicate clear biblical truths? Obviously, He wouldn't. But quite obviously, He did. I believe the reason is that **tithing is a Bible doctrine**, not just an Old Testament doctrine.

Tithing (or giving the "tenth") is mentioned no less than seven times in **Hebrews 7:1-10**. It states, "This Melchizedek was king of Salem and priest of God Most High. He met Abraham returning from the defeat of the kings and blessed him, and Abraham gave him a *tenth* of everything. First, his name means 'king of righteousness'; then also, 'king of Salem' means 'king of peace.' Without father or mother, without genealogy, without beginning of days or end of life, like the Son of God he remains a priest forever. Just think how great he was: Even the patriarch Abraham gave him a *tenth* of the plunder! Now the law requires the descendants of Levi who become priests to collect a *tenth* from the people—that is, their brothers—even though their brothers are descended from Abraham. This man, however, did not trace his descent from Levi, yet he collected a **tenth** from Abraham and blessed him who had the promises. And without doubt the lesser person is blessed by the greater. In the one case, the **tenth** is collected by men who die; but in the other case, by him who is declared to be living. One might even say that Levi, who collects the **tenth**, paid the **tenth** through Abraham, because when Melchizedek met Abraham, Levi was still in the body of his ancestor."

The point of the Hebrews passage is that Jesus is better than Melchizedek and His priesthood is far superior to that of Melchizedek's. Abraham gave tithes to Melchizedek, the representative of God, to thank Him for delivering him from his enemies. If Abraham gave a **tenth** (tithed) to Melchizedek, how much more so should we **tithe** (give a tenth) to our great High Priest, Jesus, to thank Him for all that He's done for us?

In **Matthew 22:21**, tithing is clearly implied in Jesus' answer to the Pharisees when they tried to trick Him on the subject of paying taxes. They wanted Jesus to tell them whether or not they should pay taxes to Caesar. So He asked for the coin they used for paying the tax, and they gave Him a denarius. Jesus held up the coin and asked them, "Whose portrait is this? And whose inscription?" "Caesar's," they replied. That's when Jesus said to them, "Give to Caesar what is Caesar's, and to God what is God's."

How would they know what was "Caesar's"? Simple. It would have been a percentage of their income, just as it is today with our contemporary "Caesar" — "Uncle Sam" (the U.S. Government/Internal Revenue Service). How would they know what was "God's"? Just as simple. It would have been a percentage of their income, just like it's always been: Ten percent or the tithe.

Some will erroneously say tithing was part of the Old Testament Law and, therefore, we are released from it. However, even though tithing was included as part of the Law, it was instituted hundreds of years before the Law. In Genesis 14:18-20, Abraham gave tithes to God through Melchizedek, the king-priest, 400 years before the Law was given. In Genesis 28, Jacob wakes after a dream where God spoke to him. He is so moved, he sets up a stone as a pillar and anoints it with oil. He calls the place Bethel (which means "house of God"), makes a vow to God and promises, "all that you give me I will give you a **tenth**." Hundreds of years before the Law, Jacob is expressing His love and worship to God by promising to be **a faithful tither** (giving 10% of all God gives to him).

In his book *Money Talks*, Tom Rees says, "The early church according to Origen, Jerome and Chrysostom, following the example and teaching of our Lord and the Apostles, both taught and practiced tithing. Students of Church History tell us that tithing has been practiced widely in the Christian Church since New Testament days. Tithes were recognized legally in England as early as A.D. 786, and tithing was a common practice during the reigns of Alfred, Edgar, and Canute. The Council of Trent (1545) not only enjoined payment of tithes but went so far as to excommunicate those who withheld them!"

Rees continues, "The principle of tithing is timeless. It is for every man in every age and dispensation. It was neither instituted by the dispensation of law nor terminated by the dispensation of grace. It was neither given by Moses nor abrogated by Jesus Christ. Tithing was both incorporated into the Law of Moses and into the New Testament Church."[3]

In **Matthew 5:17-18**, Jesus makes it clear He didn't come "to abolish the Law or the Prophets." Instead, He had come "to fulfill them." In other words, Jesus came to raise them to a higher standard. If you follow the entire Sermon on the Mount (Matthew 5–7), you will see Jesus making that point over and over again. For example, in **Matthew 5:21-22** He says, "You have heard that it was said to the people long ago, 'Do not murder, and anyone who murders will be subject to judgment.' But I tell you that anyone who is angry with his brother will be subject to judgment." Jesus raised the standard higher than the Law.

In **Matthew 5:27-28**, He raised the bar in regard to sexual purity. He said, "You have heard that it was said, 'Do not commit adultery.' But I tell you that anyone who looks at a woman lustfully has already committed adultery in his heart." Again, Jesus raised the standard higher than the Law.

So, if Jesus didn't come to abolish the Law or the Prophets, and He raised everything to a higher standard than had previously existed under Old Testament Law, what would that mean to us when it comes to the subject of tithing? Simple. **Tithing is not the ceiling when it comes to our giving. It's the floor.** It's where we start. Hopefully, you've already started by now. If not, why not?

Tithing is not the ceiling when it comes to our giving. It's the floor.

There's definitely something special about tithing.

Only one time in all the Bible does God say He will "throw open the floodgates of Heaven and pour out so much blessing that you will not have room enough for it." It's in Malachi 3:10. God even says we are to "test Him" and see if He'll really do it.

So what is it that activates those floodgates being opened? Is it **prayer**? Does God say if we pray every day He'll "throw open the floodgates of Heaven and pour out so much blessing that you will not have room enough for it"? **No**.

Is it **Bible study**? Does God say if we spend time studying the Bible every day that He'll "throw open the floodgates of Heaven and pour out so much blessing that you will not have room enough for it"? **No**.

Is it **witnessing**? Does God say if we will share our faith regularly with people who don't know Him, He'll "throw open the floodgates of Heaven and pour out so much blessing that you will not have room enough for it"? **No**.

Then it must be **worship**. Is that it? Does God say if we gather every week for worship and never miss it, He'll "throw open the floodgates of Heaven and pour out so much blessing that you will not have room enough for it"? **No**.

Is it **ministering to the needs of the poor**? Does God say if we'll devote our lives to helping meet the needs of the poor among us that He'll "throw open the floodgates of Heaven and pour out so much blessing that you will not have room enough for it"? **No**.

It's none of those things, even though all of those things are things we should be doing every day.

There's only one thing God says, that when we do it, it activates the floodgates of Heaven being opened and so many blessings being poured out upon us we won't have room enough for them. Are you ready for this? **That one thing is tithing.** No wonder the devil fights so hard to keep us from being tithers. He doesn't want us connected to God's continuous blessings. He doesn't want to have to dig through all of God's blessings to try to get to us so he can tempt us. He'd rather keep us disconnected from God's blessings so we are more apt to fall for his deceptions.

> *No wonder the devil fights so hard to keep us from being tithers.*

Generosity begins where tithing ends.

So, if we want to demonstrate contagious generosity, the first thing we need to do is tithe. Once we have brought God the tithe, giving 10% of whatever He blesses us with, to the storehouse—our local church—we can now give God an offering from the 90% He has given to us. Offerings are always above and beyond the tithe that belongs to God (Leviticus 27:30).

God's plan has always been to finance His work through the tithes and offerings of His people. That's how needs are met, the gospel is preached, lives are changed, and the world is impacted. That's why tithing is so important. A man came up to Wayne Smith one time and said, "'Wayne, if I don't tithe does that mean I'll go to Hell?" Wayne answered, "No, you won't go to Hell. But someone probably will."

Until we have tithed, we can't call anything we give an offering. Put simply, **generosity begins where tithing**

Generosity begins where tithing ends. Both tithing and giving offerings above the tithe are motivated by love.

ends. Both tithing and giving offerings above the tithe are motivated by love. But when we give love offerings above the tithe, we move from obedience love to blessing love. We actually bless God by moving beyond just obeying Him. Because we are doing more than we are supposed to do, giving above and beyond what He expects of us. That's why it means more to Him and results in more blessings for us.

Obedience is never extravagant because obedience is expected (Luke 17:10). That's why we need to obey and honor God first by tithing before we can bless Him with our offerings. To be sure, there are blessings for obedience. In Malachi 3:10-11, God says, "Bring the whole tithe into the storehouse, that there may be food in my house. Test me in this," says the LORD Almighty, "and see if I will not throw open the floodgates of heaven and pour out so much blessing that you will not have room enough for it. I will prevent pests from devouring your crops, and the vines in your fields will not cast their fruit." There are even greater blessings that come when we move beyond obedience and give from a heart of love.

Tithing is how you get under the spout where God's blessings come out.

In response to our obedience when it comes to tithing, God promises He will throw open the floodgates of Heaven and bury us with blessings. He also promises to protect what He gives us. Proverbs 10:22 reaffirms that, saying, "The blessing of the LORD brings wealth, and he adds no trouble to it." Our obedience will bring God's blessing and God's protection.

There are definitely specific blessings that come from being a faithful tither. Tithing is how you and I can get under the spout where God's blessings come out—all kinds of blessings, not just material or financial blessings. But the super blessings come when we give offerings above and beyond the tithe, because we are giving from the 90% God gives us, above and beyond the 10% that is set aside for Him. 100% of all we have belongs to God. So, when we give above and beyond the tithe, (beyond the 10%), it really blesses God and, in turn, He really blesses us. Giving above the tithe is when our giving becomes generous. It's also when our giving becomes contagious.

Tithing is how you can make sure what you already possess is protected.

Most people have never heard what the Bible teaches about protecting what we already possess. Yet God makes it very clear, when we trust Him and faithfully bring the tithe each week (or once a month if you are paid monthly), He will protect what we already possess.

Malachi 3:10 is the verse most people think about when they think about tithing: "'Bring the whole tithe into the storehouse, that there may be food in my house. Test me in this,' says the LORD Almighty, 'and see if I will not throw open the floodgates of heaven and pour out so much blessing that you will not have room enough for it.'" But notice what God says in the very next verse. "'I will prevent pests from devouring your crops, and the vines in your fields will not cast their fruit,' says the LORD Almighty" (Malachi 3:11). God says, "when you bring the tithe to the storehouse, I will protect what you already have."

Now, I'm sure some will say, "I don't have any crops, vines, or fields." But you probably do have a 401k, a checking account, etc. God is simply saying when we tithe, He'll protect what we already possess. Talk about a great promise. The promise of the blessings that come from tithing (i.e., the "floodgates opening up" and there being "so much blessing" that we don't have room for it) are wonderful. But it gets even better because God promises to protect what we already have. When we don't tithe, we expose everything we have and remove ourselves from the sovereign protection of Almighty God.

Once we have brought the tithe to the storehouse, whatever we give above that is an offering and is where generosity begins. It's also where the super blessings begin and where our lives and our giving become contagious.

Acts 4:32-37 is a terrific illustration of contagious generosity. "All the believers were one in heart and mind. No one claimed that any of his possessions was his own, but they shared everything they had. With great power the apostles continued to testify to the resurrection of the Lord Jesus, and much grace was upon them all. There were no needy persons among them. For from time to time those who owned lands or houses sold them, brought the money from the sales and put it at the apostles' feet, and it was distributed to anyone as he had need. Joseph, a Levite from Cyprus, whom the apostles called Barnabas (which means Son of

Encouragement), sold a field he owned and brought the money and put it at the apostles' feet."

Paul addressed the subject of giving additional offerings when he wrote to the Corinthians and encouraged them to set aside funds every time they met for worship ("on the first day of the week") so they could contribute to a special love offering which would be sent to Jerusalem (1 Corinthians 16:1-4). Obviously, this would have been above and beyond the tithes they brought, on the first day of every week, to support the ministry of their local church in Corinth.

In **2 Corinthians 8–9**, Paul wrote to the church in Corinth. He wrote about the same love offering for the poor saints in Jerusalem, thanking the Corinthians for their generosity and encouraging them to be as generous as possible to help out once again. He even referenced the fact that their giving had motivated the people in Macedonia. Evidently the generosity of the church at Corinth was contagious. Generous churches are always contagious.

Generous churches are always contagious.

In Philippians 4:10-19, Paul thanked the church at Philippi for their generosity in helping him and supporting his ministry financially. He also affirmed to them that, because of their generosity, God would meet their needs "according to His glorious riches in Christ Jesus" (Philippians 4:19b).

If we want to demonstrate contagious generosity, the first thing we need to do is be faithful tithers. The second thing we need to do is begin giving generously above the tithe to our local church. You can do that by giving above the tithe to your local church's general fund. My wife and I have

Many of the most success-ful business people in the history of our country were and are faithful tithers.

been doing that all of our married life. Every week, we give a tithe of our income and a love offering above that to our church's general fund. We have found greater joy and increased blessings by moving beyond 10% and giving even more each week to God and His church.

Many of the most successful business people in the history of our country were and are faithful tithers. William Colgate, the founder of Colgate Palmolive; Wallace Johnson, the founder of Holiday Inn; Henry Crowell, the founder of Quaker Oats; William Proctor, the founder of Proctor and Gamble; John D. Rockefeller, the founder of Standard Oil; R.G. LeTourneau, who invented the bulldozer and other massive earth-moving machines and also founded LeTourneau University; and J.C. Penney, the founder of J.C. Penney all gave the first ten percent of their income to God. Henry Crowell, J.C. Penney, and R.G. LeTourneau actually lived on 10% of their income and gave the remaining 90% away!

When you start being generous, you'll start seeing all kinds of opportunities.

You can give a love offering, above the tithe, to your church's building fund. Nearly every congregation has a building fund because every fellowship needs facilities of some kind to teach, train, and disciple people so they can send them out as missionaries into the world around us. Churches also need facilities where they can gather together for worship, instruction, and mutual encouragement in the faith (see Hebrews 10:24-25). Regardless of whether your local church has its own facilities, rents them, or shares them with someone else, your church can use love offerings to help underwrite the cost of them. This is an outstanding way to give a love offering through your local church, which in turn, will help bless and benefit untold numbers of people.

Beyond that, you may want to give love offerings towards the mission program of your local church. Every church has missions and missionaries they support. They are always in need of additional funding. If you aren't aware of your church's mission program or missionaries, call the office of your church and schedule an appointment with a staff member or leader who can help you understand the needs and direct you to the most appropriate place where your love offerings can do the most good.

Another ideal place for love offerings is to help support the youth of your church. You could give a love offering, over and above your tithe, to help send young people to church camp in the summer. Or maybe you would be interested in giving a love offering to help provide Bible college scholarships for the youth of your church to be able to attend Bible college and train for full-time leadership ministry.

Once all those needs have been met, I would recommend you ask your pastor for his input where your love offerings could best be used in the body of Christ. I'm sure he will have an endless number of suggestions for you that can benefit and bless the body of Christ. Imagine what would happen if pastors all over America were suddenly inundated with requests for appointments by faithful tithers in their local churches who wanted to give additional love offerings to

Most churches run out of resources long before they run out of dreams. However, if we can raise a generation of people who are committed to contagious generosity, we can change all that in a matter of months, maybe even weeks!

help expand the ministry of the local church and explode the Kingdom! Right now most churches run out of resources long before they run out of dreams. However, if we can raise a generation of people who are committed to contagious generosity, we can change all that in a matter of months, maybe even weeks!

Generous givers will be blessed, and those they give to will be blessed as well. It's God's cycle of continuous blessing. As long as we are generous, it never stops.

The following lines, whose author is anonymous, sum up the rewards of demonstrating contagious generosity:

Give, though your gift be small. No matter what,
    be a giver.
Remember, out of a little fount often proceeds a river.
Out of the river's many gifts, gulfs soon come to be.
Pouring their waters again and again, making a
    massive sea.
Out of the sea once again, Heaven will draw its
    showers.
And to the fount below imparts, new and refreshing
    powers.
Thus in the circle born again, brand new gifts abound.

And from the generous blessings given, far more
blessings are found.

I'm praying you'll begin to demonstrate contagious
generosity today and start the river flowing! Come on in, the
water's wonderful!

Key Points to Remember:

- The truth is, every single one of us can become generous.

- God has a way of making sure generous people can always be generous on every occasion.

- Obedience and generosity are two totally different things.

- Even though in Christ we are under grace and no longer bound by the Old Testament law, the measuring stick of "generosity" begins with the Old Testament tithe.

- Tithing is a Bible doctrine, not just an Old Testament doctrine.

- If we want to demonstrate contagious generosity, the first thing we need to do is be a faithful tither.

"If all the Christians tithed (in America) there would be no more welfare in North America. In ninety days there would be no more existing church or hospital debts. In the next ninety days, the entire world could be evangelized. There would be prayer in schools, because Christians would buy all the schools."

—Dave Ramsey

"Remember this:
Whoever sows sparingly will also reap sparingly,
and whoever sows *generously* will also reap *generously*.
Each man should give
what he has decided in his heart to give,
not reluctantly or under compulsion,
for **God loves a cheerful giver**.
And God is able to make all grace abound to you,
so that in all things at all times, having all that you need,
you will abound in every good work."
2 Corinthians 9:6-8

CHAPTER FIVE

Contagious Generosity
THE LIMITATION OF IT

Generosity is a matter of the heart. Our hearts limit our generosity or unleash it. When we say generosity is a heart matter, we're not talking about your heart muscle. But maybe we should. Just as your spiritual heart (soul) is the center of your being and directs what you do or don't do, your physical heart is located almost in the exact center of your chest between your lungs and directs virtually everything that happens in your body.

Generosity is a matter of the heart. Our hearts limit our generosity or unleash it.

Now, before you're tempted to say, "Wait a minute, I thought the brain directed what goes on in the body," let me remind you that the brain needs blood flow to operate. In fact, if blood can't get to the brain, you'll be brain-dead. Where does that blood flow come from? The heart. That means the heart is even giving life to the brain. My point is, if your heart stops or fails, it won't matter what anything else in your body is doing.

Many people believe their heart is in the left side of

their chest due to feeling a heartbeat there. That's due to the position of the heart muscle. Even though it may feel as if it's on the left, it's really almost in the center of your body. That's important because it's absolutely central to everything else going on in your body.

Your physical heart beats nearly 100,000 times a day, which comes to almost 35 million times every year. If you lived an average life that would mean your heart muscle would beat more than 2.5 billion times. Imagine that. But what's all the beating for? Your heart was designed by its Divine Creator to be generous. Generous in giving and generous in receiving. If your heart muscle ever limits its giving or stops receiving, it won't be long before you die.

Your body is designed to hold 6 quarts of blood. That blood circulates throughout your body, nonstop, three times every sixty seconds. That means, in one day, your blood will travel a distance of some 12,000 miles. Do you know how far that is? It's the equivalent of four trips across America from coast to coast. And do you know what keeps all that blood moving? Your heart muscle.

Here's the heart of the matter.

When your heart muscle ceases to be generous, it's called heart failure. Some would say you've suffered a heart attack. When that happens, if you don't receive immediate medical attention, you'll die. The same thing is true with your spiritual heart. When you cease to be generous, you are suffering spiritual

When you cease to be generous, you are suffering spiritual heart failure.

heart failure, and, if you don't receive immediate spiritual attention, you're going to die.

Our hearts determine the limits or the limitlessness of our generosity. If our hearts are right with God, do you think we'll be generous? Absolutely. That's what God created us for: to be generous. So, if you and I aren't generous, what does that mean? At the very least, it means we're having heart problems and we better do something about it.

I had just finished speaking on the subject of finances at a church when a man came up and said, "If I had your money, I'd be generous like you are." I was caught off guard but, to the best of my ability, tried to answer as graciously and yet as honestly as I could. I said, "If you were as generous as I am, you'd have my money." Generosity is not a matter of money. Rather, it's a matter of our hearts.

Generosity is a matter of your heart, not your bank account.

More money won't make anyone generous. Generosity is a matter of your heart, not your bank account. In fact, if a selfish, stingy person comes into a lot of money, they'll just be a selfish, stingy, rich person. Generosity is always a matter of the heart before it's a matter of money. Some of the most generous people I know don't have a lot of money by the world's standards. By the same token, some of the most selfish, self-centered, self-obsessed people I know, who live totally for themselves without regard for anyone else on the planet, seem to have resources running out their ears. Money won't make you anything more than what you already are. It sure won't make you generous.

Have you ever noticed how people can find money to do what they want to do and get what they want to get? But those same people will fold up like a bad clam and act like they are dirt poor when someone else has a need. Why is that? What makes them generous towards themselves but not towards others? Is it a matter of money? Absolutely not. It's a matter of the heart.

You and I are the ones who determine how generous we are. We set the limits. It has nothing to do with where we work, who we work for or work with, or how much we get paid. It has everything to do with what we've decided in our heart. That's why Paul said, "Remember this: Whoever sows sparingly will also reap sparingly, and whoever sows generously will also reap generously" (2 Corinthians 9:6). In other words, we determine the limits of our generosity, which, in turn, determines the limits of God's generosity to us.

Paul goes on to say, "Each man should give what he has decided in his heart to give, not reluctantly or under compulsion, for God loves a cheerful giver" (2 Corinthians 9:7). Paul reaffirms that generosity begins in our heart long before we reach for our wallet or checkbook. He also reaffirms that people who give with hard

Generosity begins in our heart long before we reach for our wallet or checkbook.

hearts or reluctant hearts might as well keep their money because "God loves a cheerful giver," someone who gives with inexpressible joy.

Some have incorrectly suggested that 2 Corinthians 9:7 teaches we are no longer under the biblical admonition to tithe. They point to Paul saying each man should give "what he has decided in his heart to give." But the clear context of the passage is a love offering for the poor saints in Jerusalem. It was a love offering to be given, over and above their regular giving to the local church in Corinth, to the struggling saints back in Jerusalem, and Paul encourages them to be very generous. He tells the Corinthians if they will be generous, God will be generous to them and will make sure they have more than enough so they can continue to be generous "on every occasion" (2 Corinthians 9:11c). So the extent to which generosity flows in our lives and from our lives to others is up to us.

The extent to which generosity flows in our lives and from our lives to others is up to us.

If I were a rich man . . .

Have you ever heard someone say, "If I had a million dollars I'd do some great things for the church?" I have . . . more times than I'd like to remember. If the truth were known, the majority of the people who say something like that aren't doing anything for the church with the hundred dollars they currently have. So why would they suddenly start doing something great for the church if they were to come into a huge stash of cash like a million dollars? The answer is they won't. More money won't make anyone generous. In many cases, all it does is create more problems.

Let me illustrate it for you. Several years ago, I heard about Prince Jefri Bolkiah, the favorite brother of the Sultan of Brunei. This man came into more money than you and I and everyone we know will probably ever see. Over a number of years, he accomplished what few people in the world have ever been able to do: he blew through $15 billion dollars.

How'd he do it? By building lush palaces, marinas, luxury hotels, apartment complexes, and buying thousands of cars, dozens of aircraft, and supporting his large entourage of wives, mistresses, and 35 children. Prince Jefri's money management skills, or lack thereof, threw the once incredibly wealthy nation of Brunei into a tailspin financially.

In 2000, that small country of only 330,000 people, on the northwest edge of Borneo, had to do something it previously had only heard about: work hard to earn a living. At an auction of the Prince's construction and supply company, they were able to raise $7.8 million against his monstrous mountain of debt. But, the reality is, they will probably never be able to fully recover from such a staggering financial loss, and it will most likely be many years before they ever get back to where they were before.

Times haven't always been hard for the brethren of Brunei, though. In fact, they've almost always known good times. The majority of the country has lived off the Sultan's fortunes, enjoying free education, medical care and amusement parks, employment in his oil and gas businesses as well as being able to participate in the Prince's numerous projects. And no one had to pay taxes. In exchange, the country looked the other way while the royal family played. *The New York Times* said they indulged themselves "with polo and parties, racehorses, yachts, hundreds of Rolls-Royces, and a stream of visiting starlets and beauty queens."

The article continued, "The sultan sued his brother and impounded his passport. Three months later they settled, with the prince promising to give back all of his assets and agreeing to live on a monthly allowance of $300,000. He had told a court that he really needed $500,000 to maintain his lifestyle. He is not in Brunei now to witness the dismantling of his corporation. He has chosen to spend his allowance in London and Paris, where he has not spoken about his comedown."

Still believe more money would change things for the better? Paul warned Timothy, "People who want to get rich fall into temptation and a trap and into many foolish and harmful desires that plunge men into ruin and destruction. For the love of money is a root of all kinds of evil" (1 Timothy 6:9-10a).

Before you say, "Well, if I had $15 billion dollars I would . . ." take a moment to think about what you're doing with the money you already have.

Solomon said, "Cast but a glance at riches, and they are gone, for they will surely sprout wings and fly off to the sky like an eagle" (Proverbs 23:5).

Before you say, "Well, if I had $15 billion dollars I would . . . " take a moment to think about what you're doing with the money you already have. Because if you're not managing and being generous with what you currently have, in a manner that honors the Lord, you may just find yourself in a royal mess of your own.[1]

Don't be a hog with the Lord's money.

The issue is: what are you doing with the money you already have? Are you being generous? Or are you trying to hog it all for yourself?

Someone wrote the following: "It's a common saying that a hog is good for nothing while he is alive. He can't be ridden like a horse; can't be used to draw a plow like an ox; doesn't provide clothing like sheep, nor milk like a cow; he won't guard the house like the dog. He's good only for the slaughter. So a self-centered rich man, just like a hog, does no good with his riches while he's alive. But when he is dead his riches can be used to benefit others."

Most Christians would never admit to being hogs with the Lord's money. But every survey conducted on the giving practices of evangelical church members in America tells us there are a lot of folks "pigging out" when it comes to stewardship.

Here's a good way to look at it. Take the letters **H.O.G.S.** Hogs are individuals who are **H**olding **O**nto **G**od's **S**tuff. In other words, when we hoard or hog anything, since we aren't the owner of anything on this earth, we are holding on to something that clearly belongs to God. The Bible says, "The earth is the LORD's, and everything in it, the world, and all who live in it" (Psalm 24:1). We are merely managers of the magnificent bounty of Almighty God and should never be guilty of trying to hog or hoard anything.

When Jesus told the parable of the prodigal son in Luke 15, He told about how the son took everything his father had given him and blew it on the wrong things. Jesus said the son "squandered his wealth in wild living" (Luke 15:13). Ironically, when

> *We are merely managers of the magnificent bounty of Almighty God and should never be guilty of trying to hog or hoard anything.*

he had blown through all that his father had given him, guess where he ended up? In the hog pen—with the hogs!

Jesus said, "Do not store up for yourselves treasures on earth, where moth and rust destroy, and where thieves break in and steal. But store up for yourselves treasures in heaven, where moth and rust do not destroy, and where thieves do not break in and steal" (Matthew 6:19-20). Translated: be generous, not selfish and self-centered. If we want to be continual recipients of God's bountiful blessings, we've got to be consistently generous with Him.

Jesus went on to say, "For where your treasure is, there your heart will be also" (Matthew 6:21). When we pile our treasures in the wrong place, our hearts are going to be in the wrong place. When our hearts are right with God, our treasures will be where they are supposed to be.

A heart muscle that holds on to the blood it has, refusing to give any more to the rest of the body, will bring death to the body. Likewise, Christians who hold on to what rightfully belongs to God, keeping it, hogging and hoarding it, will inevitably bring death to the body of Christ—the church.

I wonder how many churches through the years have been hopelessly hamstrung from doing what God wanted them to do because of the lack of generosity of its members? Research has repeatedly shown if the members of every church in America would tithe, it would increase the income of the church immediately and exponentially.

Imagine what could happen if all of God's people decided to move beyond obedience (tithing) to generosity? (After all, that's what God created us to be: generous givers.)

Think of the ministries that could be fully funded, the missionaries who would be fully supported, the needs that could be met, and the impact that could be made for the Kingdom. If every child of God followed God's plan when it comes to stewardship, faithfully tithing and giving beyond the tithe every week to their local church, the results would be astounding.

If every child of God followed God's plan when it comes to stewardship, the results would be astounding.

God's plan for His people has always been and always will be that we practice outrageous generosity on a regular basis. Unfortunately, too often, far too many followers of Christ fail to even come close.

If you don't do what you're supposed to do, it could bring disastrous results.

There's an old legend about an ancient village in Spain. Word came to the little village that the king was coming for a visit—something no king had ever done before. Excitement was everywhere and they decided to throw a huge celebration. All the villagers agreed to participate. But, since the village was very poor, it was decided that they would try a unique idea. Each villager was to bring a large cup of his or her best wine to the town square. Then, they would pour each of the cups of wine into a large vat and offer it to the king for his pleasure. The leaders of the village proclaimed, "When the king draws wine to drink, it will be the best wine he's ever had and he will honor our village."

The day before the king arrived, villagers came in a

steady stream, lining up to pour their cups of wine into the large vat in the village square. They were so excited to be making their "offering" for the coming king. Each villager took turns, pouring in his or her gift. After several hours, the vat was filled to the brim and the villagers cheered.

The next day, the king arrived and was brought to the square by the leaders of the village. They were so excited about the special gift they had prepared for the king. They gave him a silver chalice and encouraged him to draw out some of the wine, which represented the very best the village had. The king dipped the chalice into the vat and drank the wine. But when he drank, he turned to the leaders of the village and said, "This tastes like water, not wine." The leaders of the village quickly tasted for themselves and were stunned to find the same thing.

"What happened?" the village leaders asked one another. One by one, villagers came to their leaders and tearfully confessed what they had done. Apparently, every villager thought, "I'll keep my best wine for myself and substitute water for my gift. With all the other gifts of wine from the other villagers, the king will never know the difference." The problem was, everyone had thought the same thing, and the village dishonored the king.

When we don't give our best, it dishonors our King. In the story you just read, no one saw what those villagers put into the vat until it was too late, the king was dishonored and shame was brought upon their village. Like the villagers in the legend, when it comes to us and what we give to God, we may fool our families, our friends, and even our fellow churchgoers—no one on earth may know what we place in that offering bag when it comes down our row at church. But our King does. Jesus, sitting at the right hand of the throne of God, knows and sees everything we do, the instant we do it.

In **Mark 12:41**, the Bible says Jesus sat down "opposite the place where the offerings were put and watched the crowd putting their money into the temple treasury." Would it surprise you to know He's still watching what people give? We should make sure, regardless of what anyone else does, that we always give God our very best. We do that by tithing obediently and giving generously.

Generosity is a matter of the heart. Our hearts either limit our generosity or unleash it.

Generosity is a matter of the heart. Our hearts either limit our generosity or unleash it. What's your heart telling you to do?

Key Points to Remember:

• Our hearts determine the limits or the limitlessness of our generosity.

• Generosity is a matter of your heart, not your bank account.

• More money won't make anyone generous. In many cases, all it does is create more problems.

• Imagine what could happen if all of God's people decided to move beyond obedience (tithing) to generosity.

• When we don't give our best, it dishonors our King.

"My wife and I measure the success of the year on how much we give away. The bulk of it goes to church and related activities."

—John Grisham

Praise the LORD. Blessed is the man who fears the LORD, who
finds great delight in his commands.
His children will be mighty in the land;
the generation of the upright will be blessed.
Wealth and riches are in his house,
and his righteousness endures forever.
Even in darkness light dawns for the upright,
for the gracious and compassionate and righteous man. Good will
come to him who is *generous* and lends freely, who conducts his
affairs with justice.
Surely he will never be shaken;
a righteous man will be remembered forever.
He will have no fear of bad news; his heart is steadfast, trusting in
the LORD. His heart is secure,
he will have no fear;
in the end he will look in triumph on his foes.
Psalm 112:1-8

Chapter Six
Contagious Generosity
The Application of It

As a youngster, Michael told his dad he was going to do something special for him someday. He grew up loving basketball and was pretty good at it, too. He played at West High School in Columbus, Ohio, and was recruited by some notable coaches like Bobby Knight, Digger Phelps, George Raveling, and even Dick Vitale.

Michael said his dad, a preacher, taught him how to pray and how to play. When he was two years old, Michael said his father set up a trash can and taught him to shoot wiffle balls and rolled up socks into it. During a one-on-one game when he was fourteen, Michael said his dad knocked him to the floor trying to give him some "real life" competition. Michael recalled that in that game, he ended up beating his dad for the first time, and it was a turning point for him.

His father worked during the week at the local Pepsi-Cola plant and preached on the weekends in a small, struggling congregation. They met for a while in a storefront church located in a strip mall. Later, they moved into the basement of another church. His dad always believed that "someday" they would get to move to their own church "above ground."

Before his senior year in high school, Michael told his father, "Dad, if I get to the NBA, I'm getting you and mom a new house and a new church." Michael got better in basketball and even played at Ohio State University, leading the Big Ten in scoring as a freshman. Two years later, he made it to the NBA draft, but no one seemed to want him until the Milwaukee Bucks selected him as the 43rd pick of the 2000 draft. Most picks that low in the draft are never heard from again. But two years later, Michael had played so well he was able to sign a multiyear deal and bought his parents a house.

At the end of 2005, after leading the Milwaukee Bucks in scoring—averaging 23 points a game, which was 11th best in the NBA—Michael Redd signed a six-year deal for $91 million. One of the first things he did, instead of heading out on an extravagant spending spree for himself, was to write a check for several million dollars to help his dad's church buy a prime piece of church property on the east side of Columbus. Now, the nondenominational Philadelphia Deliverance Church has a new home which seats 500–600 worshipers. The closing took place in August, and his dad was the first person to unlock the doors of his church's new home.

Michael's dad said it "was probably one of the best moments in our life as a family." They dedicated the new church a few days later in a packed-out church service with emotions running high and Kleenex in short supply.

"Someday" finally came for Pastor James Redd . . . and what a day it must've been. Proverbs 23:24 says, "The father of a righteous man has great joy; he who has a wise son delights in him."[1] The key factor in this wonderful story is generosity, contagious generosity. A father was generous with his son and a son was generous with his dad. Both are the beneficiaries of contagious generosity. But did you notice how many others have been touched by their generosity? The ripples and ramifications go way beyond the Redd family.

Obviously, the members of Pastor Redd's church are benefiting from the contagious generosity of NBA star Michael Redd. That number will grow every week as the ministry of that church touches others. Beyond that, the story of what Michael Redd did for his father is being shared all over the

We won't know until we get to Heaven how many people were influenced by his generosity.

world, and we won't know until we get to Heaven how many people were influenced by his generosity.

What causes generosity?

Being generous causes people to be generous. In the Sermon on the Mount, Jesus said, "Which of you, if his son asks for bread, will give him a stone? Or, if he asks for a fish, will give him a snake? If you, then, though you are evil, know how to give good gifts to your children, how much more will your Father in Heaven give good gifts to those who ask him! So in everything, do to others what you would have them do for you, for this sums up the Law and the Prophets" (Matthew 7:9-12).

You may have recognized "the golden rule" in the verses above: "do to others what you would have them do for you. . . ." You and I can literally cause others to be generous by being generous ourselves. Generosity is always

When you and I choose to be generous, we can motivate and inspire others to do the same.

contagious, initiating a cycle of giving that always honors God and never stops. When you and I choose to be generous, we can motivate and inspire others to do the same.

Crises cause people to be generous. Everyone knows people respond when there's a crisis. When a tornado rips through a neighborhood, watch as total strangers give to one another like they are family members. Or an earthquake may hit and suddenly, people who have never met are embracing and comforting one another, offering their homes as a place to stay. A hurricane may hit and people from all over the country show up to help complete strangers, performing acts of kindness for free that would've cost thousands of dollars.

Crises do bring out the best in all of us, and it's wonderful to see the best in everyone. It's just sad that so often it takes a crisis to do it. A family down the street experiences a fire that completely destroys their home, so we immediately go to see if we can help. But we have to introduce ourselves because prior to the fire, we never had any interaction with our neighbor down the street.

Changed lives cause people to be generous. One of the reasons why the church of the Lord Jesus Christ is the best-funded volunteer organization in the world is this: changed lives. Other organizations can provide food, clothing, water, appliances, housing, etc. But those things only provide life enhancement. Only the church can provide life change that will last for all eternity, and that's because God has entrusted the church with the good news of the gospel. We have the glorious privilege of proclaiming that "if you confess with your mouth, 'Jesus is Lord,' and believe in your heart that God raised him from the dead, you will be saved" (Romans 10:9). Every man, woman, boy, and girl who will respond in faith, repent of their sins, and ask Jesus Christ to be their Lord and Savior can be saved (Acts 2:36-41; Ephesians 2:8-9). Romans 10:13 says, "Everyone who calls on the name of the Lord will be saved."

As your local church reaches more and more people with the gospel of Jesus Christ, you will notice an increase in giving. Not only because new believers are beginning to tithe, but also because older believers love seeing lives being changed, and it motivates them to be even more generous in their giving.

Believers love seeing lives being changed, and it motivates them to be even more generous in their giving.

A committed organization causes people to be generous. When someone finds an organization that helps meet the needs of hurting people, people become motivated to give and be generous. This would include organizations like your local church, parachurch organizations, Bible colleges, The Red Cross, The Salvation Army, Feed The Children, etc. People perceive these organizations to be first responders, on the front lines, helping hurting and needy people in our world, and they want to be a part of that, giving generously.

A cause will motivate people to be generous.
Watch what happens when people go on mission trips.
Suddenly, when they get home, they want to start doing
more for missions. Or someone goes to a summer youth
camp to serve or to help out with an inner-city outreach.
When that person gets home, he signs up to stay involved
with kids. Why? He's been captured by the cause, and that
motivates him to be generous with his time, talents, and
treasures. There are all kinds of causes in our world that
inspire and motivate people to be
generous. The greatest cause of all
is reaching people for Christ. It's
always been the greatest cause on
earth and always will be. It is the
ultimate cause, deserving our ultimate generosity.

*Reaching people for
Christ is the ultimate
cause, deserving our
ultimate generosity.*

**The love of Christ and our love for Him cause
us to be generous.** Paul wrote in 2 Corinthians 5:14, "For
Christ's love compels us." The fact that Jesus Christ loves us
is a compelling motivation for our generosity. Just recounting
all that He has done for us and how He has loved us inspires
generosity. John says, "We love because He first loved us"
(1 John 4:19). His love for us causes a reciprocal love for
Him that results in generosity. It's been said, "you can give
without loving, but you cannot love without giving." Our love
for Christ will cause us to give and to give generously.

Jesus referenced the link between our love and our generosity when He said, "For where your treasure is, there your
heart will be also" (Matthew 6:21). A few years ago, several members of our staff began to eat occasionally at a restau-

rant in our community. The manager introduced himself to us, and we began to develop a relationship with him.

Not long after that, we were in the restaurant one day talking, and the manager overheard us discussing our benevolence ministry that provides food and clothing to needy families. He asked if we would like to give those families fresh bread every week. We told him we would. So he made arrangements to have bread delivered on a regular basis to our church, and we then gave it to needy families.

As our friendship with the manager continued to grow, he said he was going to come and visit our services one day soon, which he did. He became a regular attendee and even started providing rolls and croissants for our people to enjoy on Sunday mornings. It wasn't long until I had the privilege of baptizing him and his children. Since then, they have become very active members of our church, and he has become a dear friend. It's true, "where your treasure is, there your heart will be also."

Christmas causes people to be generous. Have you ever noticed what happens to our world during the days following Thanksgiving and prior to New Year's Day? Everyone (well, almost everyone) is suddenly generous. People are generous with their time, their compliments and kind words, their baking skills, even their bank accounts. Gift giving and expressions of generosity are everywhere. There's a reason why Christmastime is called "the most wonderful time of the year." Because generosity is contagious and when everyone is being generous at the same time, it is absolutely wonderful.

Have you ever stopped to think that God wants us to

be generous all twelve months of the year, not just the month leading up to Christmas? Can you imagine what our communities and cities would be like, what our world would be like, what our churches would be like if Christmas was all year round? God created all of us to be generous and not just at certain times of the year or on certain occasions throughout the year. God has called us to be generous all the time.

Our love for others causes us to be generous. James said, "What good is it, my brothers, if a man claims to have faith but has no deeds? Can such faith save him? Suppose a brother or sister is without clothes and daily food. If one of you says to him, 'Go, I wish you well; keep warm and well fed,' but does nothing about his physical needs, what good is it? In the same way, faith by itself, if it is not accompanied by action, is dead" (James 2:14-17). Love always expresses itself in generosity to others.

John states it even stronger when he says, "If anyone has material possessions and sees his brother in need but has no pity on him, how can the love of God be in him? Dear children, let us not love with words or tongue but with actions and in truth" (1 John 3:17-18). Our love for others will cause us to be generous with them.

Generous Christians

Often people will hear a story like that of NBA star Michael Redd, and they will instantly think, "I could never do that. I don't have those kinds of resources." Obviously, most of us don't. However, we can all be generous, in ways that are so simple and easily within the reach of everyone.

So, how can you and I be generous? The opportunities are endless. Obviously we need to be generous with God and His church first. Jesus said, "Seek first his kingdom and his righteous-

We can all be generous, in ways that are so simple and easily within the reach of everyone.

ness, and all these things will be given to you as well" (Matthew 6:33). Solomon said we are to "honor the LORD" with the "firstfruits" of all our "increase" (Proverbs 3:9-10, KJV). So God needs to be first in line for our generosity. That would include a tithe of our income and love offerings beyond that. Once we have put God first, then we are ready to be generous in other ways and God promises He will help us.

There are so many other ways you and I can be generous, too. Here are just a few: We can be generous with our time, serving the needs of others through a ministry in our local church. We can use our God-given talents, gifts, and abilities to help, assist, or even lead in some area of service. We can open our home for a small group meeting, Bible study, or youth event. We can offer our vehicle to help provide transportation for outings and events or even to bring people to worship. We can be generous with our wisdom and take the time to share with a younger believer. Older believers not only should serve as role models for younger believers, but should also share their wisdom and knowledge, which can be invaluable to younger believers' growth and maturity in Christ.

We can be generous by being gracious and kind to our waiter or waitress when we are eating out, and we can leave an extra tip to express our thanks. We can send a thank-you note to someone who helps us or even just to be an encouragement to them for their unselfish acts of service on our behalf. We can offer to volunteer in someone else's place of ministry so they can have a night or weekend off and go sit with their family in a worship service. We can get a gift card and give it to a teacher, small group leader, or church staff member just to say thank you. We can buy someone a magazine or book that would encourage that person in his or her chosen vocation. We can take the time to go around and personally thank everyone we see serving in a ministry at our church. This might take a couple of weeks to do but would be a huge blessing.

We could purchase a free round of golf for a leader in our church or community just to let them know we appreciate the sacrifices they make on our behalf. We could get a gift card to a nice restaurant and give it to a senior adult couple that doesn't get out very often. We could offer to provide free babysitting to a young couple so they could have a night out. We could offer to get someone's car washed, inside and out, while he or she is working. We could offer to take someone's dry cleaning or pick it up for him or her. We could offer to clean someone's garage or even his or her house. We could get movie tickets for a young mother and her kids so they could have an afternoon out together. We could get a gift card from a clothing store so a ministry leader could purchase a new suit or new dress.

We could mow our neighbor's lawn. Better yet, we could pull the weeds in our neighbor's flower garden. We could offer to help our neighbor with his chores when we see him out in the yard some Saturday afternoon. Even if he says he doesn't need any help, the gesture of generosity will have been deposited and appreciated by your neighbor. We could purchase a new basketball or football for the neighborhood kids to replace the old one they've been using. Rather than sell our old television set or some furniture we no longer use, we could give it to a young family just getting started or to a single parent family.

Generous Churches

There are all kinds of ways we can apply the principle of contagious generosity in our individual lives. What about applying the principle of contagious generosity as a church? This is where generosity really starts to become fun. Because, with other believers, the impact of our generosity grows exponentially. Here are a few suggestions of what your church could do to apply the principle of contagious generosity in your local church.

Your church could provide scholarships for every young person so they can go to church camp in the summer. These scholarships could be partial, where the church pays half the cost, or they could be full scholarships, where your church pays the entire cost for your kids to go to church camp. This is a tremendous undertaking, but it's also a terrific investment in the young lives of your congregation.

Your church could host a "Single Parent Sunday." Our church has done this a couple of times in the last couple of years. At the close of the worship service we asked all the single parents (moms or dads) to come forward. We let them know how much we love and appreciate them. We also told them we couldn't possibly know how hard it must be to be single parents and to be doing what they're doing. Then we told them we wanted to do something tangible to express our love. So, we gave them checks for $100 each. That's one hundred dollars for each single parent and an additional $100 for each child. So if you were a single parent with four children, you received a check for $500. The moment we announced what we were doing, our congregation jumped to their feet and started cheering. It was an awesome sight! The single parents stood there, stunned, tears rolling down their cheeks, saying, "Thank you! Thank you! Thank you!" It was one of the best things we've ever done as a church. That's why we've done it more than once, and plan to keep doing things like it in the years ahead.

We excused the single parents from the service as our congregation cheered for them. We handed out the checks, privately, in our office area and the response we received from that one Sunday has been phenomenal. We received letters and emails from parents and grandparents all over the world, thanking us for loving their kids and grandkids in such a grand fashion. We received thank you notes from dozens of single parents, notes that we will keep and treasure the rest of our lives. And the positive responses are still being received in our offices.

This past fall, we gave out $200 gift cards to every single parent, every widow, and every spouse who had a mate serving in the Armed Forces anywhere in the world. Again, the response was tremendous and the blessings that come from being generous are still coming our way.

Another way for churches to apply the principle of contagious generosity is to have a missionary conference.

For this conference, invite all of your missionaries home on the same weekend so you can love on them. When we moved into our new facility, one of the first things we did was host a missions' conference where we brought every missionary we support home on the same weekend. It was a fabulous experience for everyone involved, including our missionaries. We got rooms for all of them, in a nice hotel and had hosts and hostesses take them around all weekend long. We had a first class banquet on Saturday night where we recognized each missionary, letting them know how much we love them.

We had awards made, out of crystal, for each individual missionary. (They looked like the "Golden Globe" awards.) We also gave each missionary a check for $5,000. The check was made out to them personally because we wanted to bless them and their family. We also increased our support to them. You can probably imagine the emotion of the evening as missionary after missionary stood to express their thanks for our church's love and generosity to them. It was a night I will never forget.

That weekend, we also had mission displays set up all over our facility, and our church family had a chance to visit with each missionary. Then on Sunday morning our members were able to hear from each missionary in a venue on our campus. We closed with a luncheon for our missionaries and our leaders and took a group picture with all of them together. It was the first time they had all been home to our church and the first time many of them had been given the opportunity to meet one another. It was a wonderful experience that we will definitely do again soon.

Churches can be generous by helping to meet the needs of widows and single parents when it comes to home repairs, painting, lawn care, automotive repairs, and oil changes. These activities may seem simple to us, but are difficult challenges to those living alone. Our men's ministry has an *Acts 6* ministry that covers all of these needs and does an exceptional job.

We've always held annual food and clothing drives at our church around Thanksgiving. Recently, we tried something new that really seemed to connect with our people. We purchased some grocery sacks and handed them out to our congregation the week prior to our food drive. We included a card in each sack, specifying which food items were needed. They were to bring the sacks back the next week with the items requested. The result was tremendous. Hundreds of sacks, full of food, and hundreds of people in our area had a better Thanksgiving.

Churches can begin benevolence ministries, providing food and clothing to needy families. We have a *Helping Hands* ministry on our campus. We actually remodeled a home on our property and some adjacent storage buildings, which have been ideal for use in this ministry.

Your church may also want to expand your benevolence ministry to the point where you provide furniture, appliances, and even vehicles to those who need them. There are lots of resources sitting around the homes and in the storage units of church members that could be put to good use, meeting the needs of those who would be incredibly blessed by things we no longer need or use.

God created each one of us to be givers. Generous

givers. He also wants His church to be the most generous group of people on earth. I challenge you and your church to come up with a list of cre-

I challenge you and your church to come up with a list of creative ways to apply the principle of contagious generosity in your community and get started this week.

ative ways to apply the principle of contagious generosity in your community and get started this week. When you do, you'll find yourselves being blessed continually. Contagious generosity is the key that always unlocks God's unending blessings in our lives.

A friend told me the following story recently about contagious generosity. The principal of an elementary school where my friend works has a sister who was battling cancer. At the time, she and her husband were struggling financially with medical bills and trying to provide for their children. Due to her cancer, the mother was unable to get a good night's sleep, and she and her husband decided to buy a new mattress. Since they were strapped financially, they bought the most inexpensive one they could find. It didn't help her sleep any better at all.

When the woman's husband shared this with some friends in the community, the parents at another elementary school took up a collection to help purchase a new mattress for her. Because of the generosity of those parents, a fairly large sum was collected. Another mother went to a mattress store and told the salesman about the story and how excited they were to present this gift to such a deserving family. Another man in the store overheard their conversation and identified himself as the district manager. He told her the store wanted to donate the mattress and she could pick out any mattress she wanted. So the couple was able to get one of the nicest mattresses money could buy, which helped the mother sleep much better. And, to add to the blessing, the couple was given the money originally collected for the mattress.

Generosity is always contagious. Are you?

Key Points to Remember:

- Generosity is always contagious, initiating a cycle of giving that always honors God and never stops.

- Reaching people for Christ has always been the greatest cause on earth. It deserves our ultimate generosity.

- God wants us to be generous twelve months of the year, not just the month leading up to Christmas.

- With other believers, the impact of our generosity grows exponentially.

- God created each one of us to be givers, generous givers. He also wants His church to be the most generous group of people on earth.

> "If we understood the out-of-this-world returns on our investments in others, we'd join the Macedonians and beg for the privilege of giving."
>
> —Randy Alcorn

The LORD will send a blessing on your barns and on everything you put your hand to. The LORD your God will bless you in the land he is giving you. The LORD will establish you as his holy people, as he promised you on oath, if you keep the commands of the LORD your God and walk in his ways. Then all the peoples on earth will see that you are called by the name of the LORD, and they will fear you. The LORD will grant you *abundant prosperity*—in the fruit of your womb, the young of your livestock and the crops of your ground—in the land he swore to your forefathers to give you. The LORD will open the heavens, the storehouse of his bounty, to send rain on your land in season and to *bless all the work of your hands*. You will lend to many nations but will borrow from none. The LORD will make you the head, not the tail. If you pay attention to the commands of the LORD your God that I give you this day and carefully follow them, you will always be at the top, never at the bottom. Do not turn aside from any of the commands I give you today, to the right or to the left, following other gods and serving them.

Deuteronomy 28:8-14

CHAPTER SEVEN
Contagious Generosity
THE CELEBRATION OF IT

If it were to happen today, it would ignite one of the most massive celebrations in the history of Christianity. It would be front-page news in *USA Today* and every major city newspaper. It would be the lead story on FOX News, CNN, ABC, NBC, and CBS, the featured topic on blog sites all over the world, and would likely be the most Googled subject on the Internet. It happened almost 3500 years ago but, unfortunately, most people today have still never heard about it.

Exodus 36:1-7 gives us the details. God had commissioned Moses and the Israelites to build the Tabernacle. This first-of-its-kind facility, which God designed, was going to be a dwelling place for God. God wouldn't literally come and dwell there because no place on earth—above, around, or beneath the earth—could ever contain God. Isaiah 66:1 says, "This is what the Lord says: 'Heaven is my throne, and the earth is my footstool.'" The tabernacle was going to be a holy place, a place where sin could be atoned for and where God could come and dwell with man.

God gave very specific instructions and everyone was supposed to "do the work just as the Lord has commanded." By the way, that's always the wise thing to do. God also gave people all the right skills and abilities they would need to do the work, and they began the task of constructing this special structure.

The church that gave too much.

Not only did the people do all the work on this building, but they also gave toward the cost of building. They kept giving and giving and giving until the workers actually stopped working and went to Moses with their concerns. They told Moses, "The people are bringing more than enough for doing the work the Lord commanded to be done." So Moses gave an order that was sent throughout the entire camp. "'No man or woman is to make anything else as an offering for the sanctuary.' And so the people were restrained from bringing more, because what they already had was more than enough to do all the work" (Exodus 36:6-7). Moses literally stopped the offering. He told the people, "Stop giving! We have too much already. Even if we could receive more, we could never possibly count it all or use it all."

To help give you some context for this event, you need to understand the scope and size of the congregation Moses was dealing with in Exodus 36. It would have been larger than all the megachurches in the United States and larger than any church in the world today. In the midst of this massive assembly and this

The people were restrained from bringing more, because what they already had was more than enough.

magnificent offering being received for the sacred sanctuary they were building for God, Moses stands up and says, "Stop the offering! Stop giving! We already have too much money." The Bible says the people were actually "restrained" from giving. Can you imagine that?

If that were to happen today, I guarantee you it would set off one of the greatest celebrations you and I have ever witnessed in our lives and every media outlet in the world would be there to cover it. Imagine an offering being received from God's people and the response being so huge that the pastor stands up halfway through the offering, and says, "Stop giving! We already have too much and there's no way we could ever count it or even use it."

Do it again, Lord!

Could it happen again? Not only could it happen, I believe God wants it to happen, and I also believe He has already given us the resources so it can happen. What's more, I believe He wants this type of celebration to break out in every Bible-believing church in the world. So, what would you and I have to do to get it to happen again? It's simple, actually. We have to get every Christian to practice contagious generosity: beginning with tithing from their weekly income to their local church and then giving generously above and beyond the tithe.

I believe He wants this type of celebration to break out in every Bible-believing church in the world.

As hard as it may be to believe, having an Exodus 36 type of offering like Moses and the Israelites did, is not a matter of money. It's all a matter of trust. Do we trust God and what His Word says? If we trust Him, we'll do what He says. When we do what He says, there will be a celebration of biblical proportions!

Can we trust the Bible?

The Bible is a phenomenal book. No matter what the Bible talks about, when the Bible speaks, it speaks with absolute accuracy and is accurately absolute. It is absolutely accurate scientifically, historically, and geographically. When the Bible talks about geology, biology, sociology, psychology, astronomy, botany, oceanography, or even meteorology, it is 100% absolutely accurate.

When the Bible speaks, it speaks with absolute accuracy and is accurately absolute.

Let me give you some examples:

#1 – Did you know it wasn't until the 15th century that scientists finally concluded the earth was round? Prior to that, they had always believed the earth was flat. However, over 2,000 years prior to their historic finding, Isaiah had written in Isaiah 40:22, that "God sits above the circle of the earth." If those scientists had read their Bibles, they could have saved themselves a lot of time, energy, resources, and research. Their discovery merely proved the validity and accuracy of the Bible.

#2 – Genesis 1:16 says, "God made two great lights—the greater light to govern the day and the lesser light to govern the night." The greater light is the sun (864,000 miles in diameter and 90 million miles from the earth. Scientists warn us today that the sun is shrinking. But you can relax. According to their calculations, it won't burn out for 10 billion years.). The lesser light is the moon. It merely reflects the light of the sun. The moon is 240,000 miles away from the earth. Man has walked on the moon and marveled at the dust that covers it. In actuality, that dust is made up of little, round, glass objects: titanium granules. God coated the moon with titanium granules to reflect light. It took NASA nearly 2 billion dollars to find out the moon was a reflector. Again, if they'd read their Bible, they would have found out much easier and much sooner.

In Moses' day, people believed the moon was larger than the sun. Yet, Moses called the sun the *greater* light. He didn't call it the *greatest* light. In our own galaxy, scientists tell us we have a star called Antares that is so large it could swallow 64 million suns like ours. In another constellation, there's Hercules, a star that is 100 million times bigger than Antares.

What does all that tell us? Simply, that the study of science and astronomy has merely proved, once again, the accuracy and veracity of the Word of God.

#3 – It's only been in the last few years that people have begun to talk about the earth's ozone. In fact, here in Texas, we have ozone action days. But did you know that approximately 700 years before the birth of Christ, Isaiah wrote about the ozone? In Isaiah 40:22, he wrote that God "stretches out the heavens like a canopy, and spreads them out like a tent to live in." This canopy protects man from harmful radiation from the sun. This relatively recent discovery by man merely verifies the truthfulness of the Bible.[1]

What does that have to do with the subject of contagious generosity? Everything. If the Bible can be trusted when it speaks about science and the stars, we should be able to trust the Bible when it talks about stewardship and our responsibility to be generous givers with everything God gives us.

Here's a tremendous illustration of contagious generosity, giving and receiving, from the world of science. Did you know that almost 4,000 years ago, Job wrote about the "balancing of the clouds," a fact now verified by meteorologists and scientists? Gravity pulls clouds down and warm air pushes clouds up. The annual precipitation, in the form of rain and snow that falls upon the earth, is the equivalent of 186,000 cubic miles – enough to cover the entire earth to a depth of three feet. The amount of vapor continually suspended in the air above us is estimated at 54 trillion, 460 million tons. The supply of water, above the earth, is maintained by evaporation—the constant lifting of water from the earth up into the atmosphere—which is all accomplished by the sun. See the cycle of giving and receiving and the principle of contagious generosity at work?

If the Bible can be trusted when it speaks about science and the stars, we should be able to trust the Bible when it talks about stewardship

All of this is kept in perfect balance by God and was written in the Word of God almost 4,000 years ago. The discoveries made by scientists, doctors, researchers, archaeologists, and meteorologists merely serve to confirm what we already know: The Bible is absolutely accurate and accurately absolute.[2]

So when the Bible speaks about the subject of steward-ship and managing the resources God gives us in a manner that honors Him by being generous givers, we know the Bible can be trusted. We're not going to get burned. We're going to get blessed. Proverbs 10:22 says, "The blessing of the LORD brings wealth, and he adds no trouble to it." The Psalmist tells us the "blessed man . . . yields fruit in season and [his] leaf does not wither. Whatever he does prospers . . . For the LORD watches over the way of the righteous but the way of the wicked will perish" (Psalm 1:1-6).

The best investment you can ever make.

America is a generous nation. Following the terrorist attack on September 11, 2001, our country rallied together like never before and contributed $2.8 billion to help our fel-low Americans. In 2005, what some are calling the worst year ever for natural disasters, Americans gave $1.78 billion to help those affected by the devastating tsunami in Southeast Asia and Indonesia, and an additional $78 million to those who suffered the horrific earthquakes in Kashmir. The response of Americans to Hurricane Katrina represented the largest private response to any single event in our nation's history with contributions totaling over $3 billion.

That's phenomenal generosity! But it doesn't even come close to the resources that would be immediately available to the church of the Lord Jesus Christ if every person who's a Christian began to tithe faithfully and give generously to his or her local church every week. What's even more astound-ing is how many more people could be reached for Christ, how many churches would be standing room only, how many Bible colleges would be bursting at the seams with students, how many missions would have more workers than ever, and how many ministries would be transforming communities because they suddenly had the resources to do everything God called them to do.

So what should we be doing with our wealth? In Luke 16:9, Jesus said, "I tell you, use worldly wealth to gain friends for yourselves. So that when it is gone, you will be welcomed into eternal dwellings." Jesus said we are to use our money to invest in the lives of men, women, boys, and girls so that when our money is gone, and we have gone to Heaven, there will be all kinds of people there, greeting and thanking us for making a difference in their lives through our generosity. Jesus said using our wealth to reach people with the gospel is the best investment we can ever make.

Jesus said using our wealth to reach people with the gospel is the best investment we can ever make.

Ordinary People, Extraordinary Gifts

You don't have to wait until you amass vast sums of money to be generous. You can be generous right now. When it comes to contagious generosity, it's not a matter of how much you make, but what you do with what you already have. One story that really inspires me when it comes to generosity is the story of Mr. C. J. Teubert from Huntington, West Virginia. Mr. Teubert never made more than $6,000 a year during his career as a postal worker. He used to wear second-hand clothes and scribbled out his last will and testament on the back of an old business letter. But when he died at the age of 91 back in 1979, he left behind an estate worth more than $3 million dollars, most of which he gave to the American Foundation for the Blind. That gift will keep on giving forever. Talk about generosity that's contagious.

Another terrific example of generosity not being a matter of how much money you make, but what you do with what you already have, comes from a Tennessee preacher named Vertrue Sharp. He was the former pastor at Middle-Settlements United Methodist Church in Maryville, Tennessee. His sister said he "saved every penny he made" and his desire was to help the needy. When he died, they said even though he was a pastor who "lived like a pauper," he left behind "the estate of a king." According to the *Knoxville News-Sentinel*, his estate was worth almost $2 million. More than $500,000 of that was designated in gifts to two hospitals, some of which would be used by chaplains to create programs for cancer patients and their families. Again, this reveals generosity that's absolutely contagious.

John Wesley said, "Make all you can, save all you can, give all you can." You and I should do everything we can to earn as much as we can, so we can give as much as we can. One of my favorite authors, Randy Alcorn, says,

> *I'm convinced when you and I begin giving more, God will bless us more, and we'll have more to give.*

"God prospers me not to raise my standard of living, but to raise my standard of giving." I'm convinced when you and I begin giving more, God will bless us more, and we'll have more to give.

Extraordinary Wealth, Expanding Generosity

According to Forbes, which tracks the assets of the super wealthy, there are now 691 billionaires on earth with a total net worth of over $2.2 trillion dollars. That's $300 billion more than the super wealthy had one year ago.[3] The truth is, though, more wealth doesn't always translate into more generosity. Bill Gates, considered the richest man in the world with $46.5 billion, has been quoted as saying, "It's harder to give the money away than it is to make it." That's because once we get money in our hands, there's a strong tendency to start thinking it's ours. Thankfully, Bill and Melinda Gates top the list of the 50 Most Generous Philanthropists, having given over $10 billion to charitable causes and institutions in the last five years.[4]

The encouraging news is that there are multitudes of people in our world who are raising the standard of giving by their contagious generosity and some of them are among the richest people in the world. In the January 2006 issue, *New Man* magazine did a brief profile on four men who are on the Forbes' list of "The 400 Richest People in America." According to the article, these four men have a combined net worth of approximately $14 billion and are "laying up treasures in heaven." Their generosity is impacting and inspiring our world.[5]

The article profiled Richard DeVos from Ada, Michigan, one of the co-founders of Amway (which has been renamed Alticor), who recently gave $1 million to hurricane relief. Philip Anschutz from Denver, also included in the article, owns the Walden Media company which recently released the blockbuster movie *The Chronicles of Narnia: The*

Lion, the Witch and the Wardrobe. Also included was Drayton McLane, from Temple, Texas, owner of the Houston Astros, a major benefactor for Baylor University who is involved with Major League Baseball's Chapel Ministry. And David Green, founder of Hobby Lobby, who keeps all of his stores closed on Sundays and has donated millions of dollars to world missions, was included as well.

According to *Business Week*, in a special report on philanthropy, "experts say the ranks of the mega-givers are sure to grow, especially as the largest intergenerational wealth transfer in history looms on the horizon, with at least $41 trillion estimated to change hands by 2052—$6 trillion of which is projected to go to charity, according to Boston College's John J. Havens and Paul G. Schervish. Even the most youthful on the Top 50 are participating in the acceleration and mega-gift trends."[6]

In January of 2006, the largest single gift ever given in the history of the NCAA was given to Oklahoma State University in Stillwater, Oklahoma. Billionaire alumnus, T. Boone Pickens, gave $165 million to the athletic program at OSU. His gift tops the previous largest donation, which had been given by former Las Vegas casino owner, Ralph Engelstad, to the University of North Dakota in 1998. The gift from Mr. Pickens, a 77-year-old Texas oil tycoon with a net worth of $1.5 billion, will be used to help create an athletic village and update a stadium that already bears his name.

While generosity of that size may appear rare to most people, the truth is, there are tens of thousands of people here in America who could make similar gifts this week if they decided to be generous. Wouldn't it be wonderful to see

Wouldn't it be won-
derful to see multi-
million-dollar gifts
to local churches?

a number of multimillion-dollar gifts, given to local churches by Christians who've been blessed with large amounts of wealth? T. Boone Pickens' gift will be used for fun and games that won't last. A similar gift to a local church could be used to reach thousands of people with the gospel of Jesus Christ, and the impact of that gift would last for all eternity.

There are significantly wealthy Christians all over America who have been generously blessed by God, maybe not to the level of T. Boone Pickens—maybe more. Here's my challenge. If you are one of those people who has been financially blessed by God, with resources most people can only dream of, let me challenge you to make a gift to your local church this week. Give a gift that will absolutely accelerate the outreach, impact, and influence of your church beyond anyone's wildest dreams.

There are Christian people in our churches today who can donate entire buildings, eliminate a local church's remaining indebtedness, help fund staff additions, underwrite entire mission projects, you name it. I'm asking you, if you are one of those individuals, or one of those families, to step out in faith and do something outrageously generous for your local church. I can promise you, your generosity will be contagious, will stimulate the generosity of others in your congregation, and will influence others all around the world to do the same. When you give a gift like that, send me a note at the address provided in the back of this book. I'd love to hear your story and, with your permission, would like to share it in a future book.

If you and I want to be the recipients of God's continuous blessings, we've got to become generous. We weren't created to keep anything. We were created to give everything—and to give generously. But remember, generosity and a generous lifestyle are about so much more than money. Don't limit your generosity just to your finances. We need to be generous with our time, our talents, our gifts, and our abilities. We need to be generous in serving others. We need to be generous in extending forgiveness to others. We need to be generous in our love for the Lord. In short, we need to be generous in every area of our lives.

Don't limit your generosity just to your finances.

Regardless of where you are today when it comes to generosity, I'm praying you'll accept the challenge to become even more generous. I'm praying God will use you and me to start an epidemic of generosity that won't end until Jesus comes. I'm praying we'll infect each other and everyone who knows us. My prayer is we'll spread the generosity germ to everyone we come in contact with and that Christians and churches all over the world will catch it. I'm praying we'll become contagious! Will you make that your prayer, too?

Remember the story of Mary anointing Jesus with that bottle of perfume that cost a full year's wages? There will always be a Judas who will say you're overdoing it. There will always be someone who will tell you, "You don't want to take this generosity deal too far." Well, God did . . . and He still is!

An Explosion of Contagious Generosity

You and I are in the beginning stages of an unstoppable explosion of contagious generosity in churches all over America and the world. How do I know? Because of the huge numbers of people and churches that are catching the vision of being faithful tithers and giving beyond the tithe every week. Vast numbers of Christians are doing a better job of managing their money by following biblical princi-ples, moving toward being debt free, and committing themselves to lifestyles of contagious generosity. Be-cause of that, we are mov-ing into what promises to be one of the most, if not the most, exciting periods in the history of the church.

We are moving into what promises to be one of the most, if not the most, exciting periods in the history of the church.

Would you like to be a part of that? Then commit your-self to a lifetime of contagious generosity. Not only will you be doing what God created you to do, but you will also find yourself buried beneath so many blessings you can't possibly keep them all. The key to receiving God's continuous bless-ings is to keep giving and giving and giving and . . .

The curse can be reversed.

Many have called it the most famous curse in history and say it began back in 1920. That's when the Boston Red Sox received $125,000 for a left-handed pitcher they traded to the New York Yankees. Actually, it was Harry Frazee, then owner of the Boston Red Sox, who is credited with the infamous decision of trading the team's star, George Herman Ruth, also known as "The Babe," to their arch rivals.

When the trade took place, the Red Sox had already won five World Series titles. Their rivals, the Yankees, had yet to win their first. From that day until now however, the Yankees have won baseball's World Series twenty-six times. And the Red Sox? They haven't won a single time. In fact, each time they got close—in 1946, 1967, 1975, and 1986—they lost. It appeared to everyone that the Red Sox really were under a curse. Until now.

In 2004, the Red Sox had a phenomenal season with a record of 98 wins and 64 losses. But no one predicted how remarkable their season would be. They went on to win the American League Division Series against the Anaheim Angels. Then they made history by defeating their perennial adversary, the Yankees, becoming the first team ever to rally from a 3-0 deficit and win the American League Championship Series.

On October 27, 2004, the Boston Red Sox finally broke "the curse of the Bambino," winning the World Series by defeating the St. Louis Cardinals in four straight games. For eighty-six years (31,458 days), the Red Sox lived with a curse and without a World Series Championship.

Were the Boston Red Sox under a genuine curse all those years? We may never know. One thing we do know is there are millions of people living under an absolutely authentic curse today. Not a legendary one, but a legitimate one. Not a fabled one, but a factual one.

This time the curse is not reserved for a baseball team in Massachusetts, but rather a massive number of people scattered all over the earth who call themselves Christians. This curse does not originate in some mythological mystique. Rather, it comes from the Creator of the Universe—the God of Heaven and earth. The curse is bigger than any ball game, ballpark, and ball team on earth, with ramifications that are world serious.

Malachi 3:8-10 gives the details. "'Will a man rob God? Yet you rob me. But you ask, "How do we rob you?" In tithes and offerings. You are under a curse—the whole nation of you—because you are robbing me. Bring the whole tithe into the storehouse, that there may be food in my house. Test me in this,' says the LORD Almighty, 'and see if I will not throw open the floodgates of heaven and pour out so much blessing that you will not have room enough for it.'"

We need to step up to the plate, every week of our lives, and trust God.

We need to step up to the plate, every week of our lives, and trust God when it comes to our finances by being faithful tithers: giving ten percent of our income back to God, and giving beyond that in offerings to Him as well. When we do, the curse will be lifted and the blessings will start to fall in floodgate fashion.

ESPN won't tell you this, but the real champions in our world are tithers and individuals who give beyond the tithe every week to the work of God through His church.

Once you start tithing and giving above and beyond, you'll quickly discover three things: (1) the ever-increasing, unending bounty of God's blessings; (2) you can't and won't outgive God no matter how much you try; and (3) He's not after your money; it's already His—all of it. The latter leads to perhaps the greatest discovery of all . . . He just wants to bless your socks off![7]

Oh, and one more thing . . . when you start being continually generous, you're going to find yourself the beneficiary of God's continuous blessings.

. . . You're also going to be contagious!

"God is generous and never runs out of blessings.
God delights in giving—
it's what He does best."

Eugene Peterson[8]

Key Points to Remember:

- Imagine an offering being received from God's people and the response being so huge that the pastor stands up halfway through the offering and says, "Stop giving!"

- If the Bible can be trusted when it speaks about science and the stars, we should be able to trust the Bible when it talks about stewardship.

- The Bible can be trusted. We're not going to get burned. We're going to be blessed.

- When it comes to contagious generosity, it's not a matter of how much you make, but what you do with what you already have.

- The real champions in our world are tithers and individuals who give beyond the tithe every week to the work of God through His church.

"If you will invest in winning the lost, God will give you abundance you cannot contain."

—John Hagee

No one is to appear before me empty-handed.
Exodus 23:15

Charity, to be fruitful, must cost us.
—Mother Teresa

Behold, I am coming soon!
My reward is with me, and I will give to everyone
according to what he has done.
—Jesus
Revelation 22:12

We are rich only through what we give;
and poor only through what we keep.
—Anne Sophie Swetchine

Earn as much as you can. Save as much as you can.
Invest as much as you can. Give as much as you can.
—John Wesley

There never was a person who did anything worth doing, who
did not receive more than he gave.
—Henry Ward Beecher

One of the best discoveries you will ever make
is to learn that God wants you to use His wealth
to finance His kingdom. It's not our wealth,
and it's not for us. It's God's wealth,
and we are to be good stewards,
using it to help build His kingdom.
—Barry L. Cameron[9]

ENDNOTES

Chapter One

1. David Cay Johnston, *New York Times*, December 19, 2005.

2. George Barna, *The Barna Update*, April 5, 2000; **www.barna.org**.

Chapter Two

1. Barry L. Cameron, The *CCCWeekly*, December 16, 2002 (Grand Prairie, TX 75052: Crossroads Christian Church); **http://www.crossroadschristian.net**.

Chapter Three

1. Barry L. Cameron, The *CCCWeekly*, October 21, 2002 (Grand Prairie, TX 75052: Crossroads Christian Church); **http://www.crossroadschristian.net**.

Chapter Four

1. Barry L. Cameron, The *CCCWeekly*, July 5, 2004 (Grand Prairie, TX 75052: Crossroads Christian Church); **http://www.crossroadschristian.net**.

2. Edward Veith, "Who Gives Two Cents for Missions?" *World Magazine* 20 (October 22, 2005).

3. Tom Rees, *Money Talks* (Otford Hills, Sevenoaks, Kent, England: Hildenborough Hall, n.d.) 33.

Chapter Five

1. Barry L. Cameron, The *CCCWeekly*, November 6, 2001 (Grand Prairie, TX 75052: Crossroads Christian Church); **http://www.crossroadschristian.net**.

Chapter Six

1. Barry L. Cameron, The *CCCWeekly*, December 18, 2005 (Grand Prairie, TX 75052: Crossroads Christian Church); **http://www.crossroadschristian.net**.

Chapter Seven

1. Barry L. Cameron, The *CCCWeekly*, December 6, 1999 (Grand Prairie, TX 75052: Crossroads Christian Church); http://www.crossroadschristian.net.

2. Ibid.

3. "The World's Billionaires," *Forbes.com* (March 10, 2005); http://www.forbes.com.

4. "The 50 Most Generous Philanthropists," *BusinessWeek Online* (November 29, 2004); http://www.businessweek.com.

5. *New Man Magazine*, January/February 2006 (Lake Mary, FL, 32746: Strang Communications); http://www.newmanmagazine.com.

6. "The Top Givers," *BusinessWeek Online* (November 29, 2004); http://www.businessweek.com.

7. Barry L. Cameron, The *CCCWeekly*, November 7, 2004 (Grand Prairie, TX 75052: Crossroads Christian Church); http://www.crossroadschristian.net.

8. Eugene Peterson, *Are You Talking to Me, God?* (Nashville: J. Countryman, 2004) 81.

9. Barry Cameron, *The ABC's of Financial Success Workbook* (Joplin, MO: HeartSpring, 2002) 69.

Appendix

Questions about Tithing, Giving & Generosity

Should I tithe off my gross or net income?

This is one of the most frequently asked questions. The answer I always give is, "What would you like to be blessed on? Your net or your gross?" My wife and I tithe off everything God gives us. We have tithed from tax refunds, though we had already previously tithed off that money. Why? We love being blessed.

Shouldn't I pay my bills first?

No. Nothing should ever come before God. The very first check we write, every time we get paid, should be to God. Jesus promised in Matthew 6:33, that if we put God first, He'll take care of everything else in our lives. That's what Lordship is all about. If we put anyone or anything ahead of God, we're on our own to meet our needs. God needs to be first in every area of our lives, especially in the area of giving. When we put God first, we will always have enough for Uncle Sam, Aunt Martha, Visa, MasterCard, and the mortgage company. When we put anything else ahead of God, we'll never have enough.

What if I get paid monthly? Should I tithe once a month or divide it up each week?

If you get a paycheck once a month, I would recommend you write out your tithe check (remember the principle of "Honoring the Lord with our firstfruits"), along with a generous love offering, as soon as you get paid. You should place your check in the offering on the very next Sunday. The remaining Sundays of the month, you can give an offering.

When should I give?

Every chance you get! Obviously, you should tithe everything God blesses you with and every time God blesses you. If you get a raise, a bonus, a birthday gift, an insurance refund, etc., always give God 10%. Beyond that, you should give every time you worship. We sing every time we worship. We pray every time we worship. We read the Scripture every time we worship. We participate in everything else every time we worship. Why wouldn't we participate in the offering? As you develop a lifestyle of contagious generosity, you'll start viewing offering time as one of the most rewarding parts of every worship experience.

How should I give? Cash or check?

You should always give by check when you are giving your tithe or a love offering. This makes it easier for those entrusted to count the offering. It also eliminates any confusion over who gave what and removes the temptation from anyone counting or recording to take something from an offering.

Where should I give?

The primary place for your giving should always be your local church. Both your tithe and the majority of your offerings should go to your local church where you are fed. We don't eat at McDonald's and give at Burger King.

What about using giving envelopes?

If your church has giving envelopes available for you, use them. Giving envelopes make it very convenient in giving. They also serve as a reminder as you prepare to give each week.

What if I have to be gone on a Sunday?

If you are going out of town on business or on vacation, make sure your tithe and offerings are turned in for the period you will be gone. You can either mail it in to the church office or drop it off before you leave. The financial needs and responsibilities of your church occur 365 days a year. Consistent giving every week by the members of your church enables your church to accomplish what God has called them to do all year long.

When you have to be gone from your home church on a particular Sunday, find a Bible-believing church where you are going so you can have a place to worship. Prepare before you go so you can share in their offering, too. You will bless the church where you are worshiping and will receive a blessing as well for your generosity.

When I give to a special offering, should I use my tithe for that?

No. First of all, the tithe belongs to God, not us. So we aren't free to divide it or designate it. It goes to the "storehouse," which is the local church. Until we have given the tithe, whatever we give can't be considered an offering. We can't "offer" what we "owe." Tithing is a matter of obedience. Generosity is a matter of giving more than is expected. So, when you give to a special offering, it always needs to be above and beyond the tithe you give each week to your local church.

Is it wise to be giving offerings for buildings? Shouldn't that money be used for missions?

Yes and no. Yes, we should be giving offerings for buildings. God didn't build the tabernacle or the temple in the Old Testament, but He did design both of those structures and gave specific instructions on how they were to be built and how His people were to give to support them (Exodus 25:1-40:38; 1 Chronicles 28:1-21, especially verse 19; 1 Chronicles 29:1-25).

The second part of the question deals with missions giving versus giving for buildings. Rather than do one or the other, we should do both. By building facilities for worship and ministry, we can reach more people, which will result in more being given for missions. However, if we decide not to build any facilities and instead, give all that money to missions, it would result in a one-time blessing followed by nothing because churches can't keep growing and reaching people if there is no place to meet, teach, train, disciple, and send. Missionaries depend on local churches for support. Therefore, we should do both. Build as many strong churches as we possibly can, and strongly support as many mission works as possible.

Doesn't the Bible, specifically Matthew 6:1-4, teach that our giving should be in secret?

No. The context of Matthew 6:1-4 is giving to the needy (i.e., giving to the poor, widows, orphans, etc.) not tithing or giving offerings for the work of God. The larger context of Jesus' remarks in Matthew 6 was the hypocrisy of the Pharisees who were doing good deeds to be seen of men. Jesus was saying, when we give to the needy, we aren't to "trumpet" our generosity to others. Instead, we should keep that to ourselves. Because if we seek the praise of men for our generosity to the needy, we already have our reward (Matthew 6:2).

As for giving publicly, King David shared what he had given publicly and the people rejoiced as they watched their leaders give publicly for the building of the temple (1 Chronicles 29:1-25). At the temple, Jesus watched as people gave publicly (Mark 12:41-44; Luke 21:1-4). The early church was known for giving in the presence of others (Acts 4:32-37). Ananias and Sapphira were struck dead publicly because they lied about what they had given in the presence of others (Acts 5:1-11).

Examples of Offerings & Giving in the Bible

Offerings for the Tabernacle

Exodus 25:2-9

"Tell the Israelites to bring me an offering. You are to receive the offering for me from each man whose heart prompts him to give. These are the offerings you are to receive from them: gold, silver and bronze; blue, purple and scarlet yarn and fine linen; goat hair; ram skins dyed red and hides of sea cows; acacia wood; olive oil for the light; spices for the anointing oil and for the fragrant incense; and onyx stones and other gems to be mounted on the ephod and breastpiece. Then have them make a sanctuary for me, and I will dwell among them. Make this tabernacle and all its furnishings exactly like the pattern I will show you."

Exodus 30:11-16

Then the LORD said to Moses, "When you take a census of the Israelites to count them, each one must pay the LORD a ransom for his life at the time he is counted. Then no plague will come on them when you number them. Each one who crosses over to those already counted is to give a half shekel, according to the sanctuary shekel, which weighs twenty gerahs. This half shekel is an offering to the LORD. All who cross over, those twenty years old or more, are to give an offering to the LORD. The rich are not to give more than a half shekel and the poor are not to give less when you make the offering to the LORD to atone for your lives. Receive the atonement money from the Israelites and use it for the service of the Tent of Meeting. It will be a memorial for the Israelites before the LORD, making atonement for your lives."

Exodus 36:1-7

So Bezalel, Oholiab and every skilled person to whom the LORD has given skill and ability to know how to carry out all the work of constructing the sanctuary are to do the work just as the LORD has commanded. Then Moses summoned Bezalel and Oholiab and every skilled person to whom the LORD had given ability and who was willing to come and do the work. They received from Moses all the offerings the Israelites had brought to carry out the work of constructing the sanctuary. And the people continued to bring freewill offerings morning after morning. So all the skilled craftsmen who were doing all the work on the sanctuary left their work and said to Moses, "The people are bringing more than enough for doing the work the LORD commanded to be done." Then Moses gave an order and they sent this word throughout the camp: "No man or woman is to make anything else as an offering for the sanctuary." And so the people were restrained from bringing more, because what they already had was more than enough to do all the work.

Offerings for the Temple

1 Chronicles 29:1-25

Then King David said to the whole assembly: "My son Solomon, the one whom God has chosen, is young and inexperienced. The task is great, because this palatial structure is not for man but for the LORD God. With all my resources I have provided for the temple of my God—gold for the gold work, silver for the silver, bronze for the bronze, iron for the iron and wood for the wood, as well as onyx for the settings, turquoise, stones of various colors, and all kinds of fine stone and marble—all of these in large quantities. Besides, in my devotion to the temple of my God I now give my personal treasures of gold and silver for the temple of my God, over and above everything I have provided for this holy temple: three thousand talents of gold (gold of Ophir) and seven thousand talents of refined silver, for the overlaying of the walls of the buildings, for the gold work and the silver work, and for all the work to be done by the craftsmen. Now, who is willing to consecrate himself today to the LORD?"

Then the leaders of families, the officers of the tribes of Israel, the commanders of thousands and commanders of hundreds, and the officials in charge of the king's work gave willingly. They gave toward the work on the temple of God five thousand talents and ten thousand darics of gold, ten thousand talents of silver, eighteen thousand talents of bronze and a hundred thousand talents of iron. Any who had precious stones gave them to the treasury of the temple of the LORD in the custody of Jehiel the Gershonite. The people rejoiced at the willing response of their leaders, for they had given freely and wholeheartedly to the LORD. David the king also rejoiced greatly.

David praised the LORD in the presence of the whole assembly, saying,

"Praise be to you, O LORD,

God of our father Israel,
from everlasting to everlasting.

Yours, O LORD, is the greatness and the power
and the glory and the majesty and the splendor;
for everything in heaven and earth is yours.

Yours, O LORD, is the kingdom;
you are exalted as head over all.

Wealth and honor come from you;
you are the ruler of all things.

In your hands are strength and power
to exalt and give strength to all.

Now, our God, we give you thanks,
and praise your glorious name.

"But who am I, and who are my people, that we should be able to give as generously as this? Everything comes from you, and we have given you only what comes from your hand. We are aliens and strangers in your sight, as were all our forefathers. Our days on earth are like a shadow, without hope. O LORD our God, as for all this abundance that we have provided for building you a temple for your Holy Name, it comes from your hand, and all of it belongs to you. I know, my God, that you test the heart and are pleased with integrity. All these things have I given willingly and with honest intent. And now I have seen with joy how willingly your people who are here have given to you. O LORD, God of our fathers Abraham, Isaac and Israel, keep this desire in the hearts of your people forever, and keep their hearts loyal to you. And give my son Solomon the wholehearted devotion to keep your commands, requirements and decrees and to do

everything to build the palatial structure for which I have provided."

Then David said to the whole assembly, "Praise the LORD
your God." So they all praised the LORD, the God of their
fathers; they bowed low and fell prostrate before the LORD
and the king.

The next day they made sacrifices to the LORD and presented burnt offerings to him: a thousand bulls, a thousand
rams and a thousand male lambs, together with their drink
offerings, and other sacrifices in abundance for all Israel.
They ate and drank with great joy in the presence of the LORD
that day.

Then they acknowledged Solomon son of David as king
a second time, anointing him before the LORD to be ruler and
Zadok to be priest. So Solomon sat on the throne of the LORD
as king in place of his father David. He prospered and all
Israel obeyed him. All the officers and mighty men, as well
as all of King David's sons, pledged their submission to King
Solomon.

The LORD highly exalted Solomon in the sight of all Israel
and bestowed on him royal splendor such as no king over
Israel ever had before.

2 Chronicles 24:1-16

Joash was seven years old when he became king, and he
reigned in Jerusalem forty years. His mother's name was
Zibiah; she was from Beersheba. Joash did what was right in
the eyes of the LORD all the years of Jehoiada the priest.
Jehoiada chose two wives for him, and he had sons and

daughters. Some time later Joash decided to restore the temple of the LORD. He called together the priests and Levites and said to them, "Go to the towns of Judah and collect the money due annually from all Israel, to repair the temple of your God. Do it now." But the Levites did not act at once.

Therefore the king summoned Jehoiada the chief priest and said to him, "Why haven't you required the Levites to bring in from Judah and Jerusalem the tax imposed by Moses the servant of the LORD and by the assembly of Israel for the Tent of the Testimony?"

Now the sons of that wicked woman Athaliah had broken into the temple of God and had used even its sacred objects for the Baals.

At the king's command, a chest was made and placed outside, at the gate of the temple of the LORD. A proclamation was then issued in Judah and Jerusalem that they should bring to the LORD the tax that Moses the servant of God had required of Israel in the desert. All the officials and all the people brought their contributions gladly, dropping them into the chest until it was full. Whenever the chest was brought in by the Levites to the king's officials and they saw that there was a large amount of money, the royal secretary and the officer of the chief priest would come and empty the chest and carry it back to its place. They did this regularly and collected a great amount of money. The king and Jehoiada gave it to the men who carried out the work required for the temple of the LORD. They hired masons and carpenters to restore the LORD's temple, and also workers in iron and bronze to repair the temple.

The men in charge of the work were diligent, and the

repairs progressed under them. They rebuilt the temple of God according to its original design and reinforced it. When they had finished, they brought the rest of the money to the king and Jehoiada, and with it were made articles for the LORD's temple: articles for the service and for the burnt offerings, and also dishes and other objects of gold and silver. As long as Jehoiada lived, burnt offerings were presented continually in the temple of the LORD.

Now Jehoiada was old and full of years, and he died at the age of a hundred and thirty. He was buried with the kings in the City of David, because of the good he had done in Israel for God and his temple.

Offerings for the needy

Acts 2:44-47

All the believers were together and had everything in common. Selling their possessions and goods, they gave to anyone as he had need. Every day they continued to meet together in the temple courts. They broke bread in their homes and ate together with glad and sincere hearts, praising God and enjoying the favor of all the people. And the Lord added to their number daily those who were being saved.

Romans 15:26-27

For Macedonia and Achaia were pleased to make a contribution for the poor among the saints in Jerusalem. They were pleased to do it, and indeed they owe it to them. For if the Gentiles have shared in the Jews' spiritual blessings, they owe it to the Jews to share with them their material blessings.

Offerings to help meet the needs of fellow believers

Acts 4:32-37

All the believers were one in heart and mind. No one claimed that any of his possessions was his own, but they shared everything they had. With great power the apostles continued to testify to the resurrection of the Lord Jesus, and much grace was upon them all. There were no needy persons among them. For from time to time those who owned lands or houses sold them, brought the money from the sales and put it at the apostles' feet, and it was distributed to anyone as he had need. Joseph, a Levite from Cyprus, whom the apostles called Barnabas (which means Son of Encouragement), sold a field he owned and brought the money and put it at the apostles' feet.

1 Corinthians 16:1-4

Now about the collection for God's people: Do what I told the Galatian churches to do. On the first day of every week, each one of you should set aside a sum of money in keeping with his income, saving it up, so that when I come no collections will have to be made. Then, when I arrive, I will give letters of introduction to the men you approve and send them with your gift to Jerusalem. If it seems advisable for me to go also, they will accompany me.

Offerings for missions

Acts 11:29-30

The disciples, each according to his ability, decided to provide help for the brothers living in Judea. This they did, sending their gift to the elders by Barnabas and Saul.

2 Corinthians 8:16-21

I thank God, who put into the heart of Titus the same concern I have for you. For Titus not only welcomed our appeal, but he is coming to you with much enthusiasm and on his own initiative. And we are sending along with him the brother who is praised by all the churches for his service to the gospel. What is more, he was chosen by the churches to accompany us as we carry the offering, which we administer in order to honor the Lord himself and to show our eagerness to help. We want to avoid any criticism of the way we administer this liberal gift. For we are taking pains to do what is right, not only in the eyes of the Lord but also in the eyes of men.

Giving Generously

2 Corinthians 9:6-11

Remember this: Whoever sows sparingly will also reap sparingly, and whoever sows generously will also reap generously. Each man should give what he has decided in his heart to give, not reluctantly or under compulsion, for God loves a cheerful giver. And God is able to make all grace abound to you, so that in all things at all times, having all that you need, you will abound in every good work. As it is written: "He has scattered abroad his gifts to the poor; his righteousness endures forever." Now he who supplies seed to the sower and bread for food will also supply and increase your store of seed and will enlarge the harvest of your righteousness. You will be made rich in every way so that you can be generous on every occasion, and through us your generosity will result in thanksgiving to God.

1 Timothy 6:17-19

Command those who are rich in this present world not to be arrogant nor to put their hope in wealth, which is so uncertain, but to put their hope in God, who richly provides us with everything for our enjoyment. Command them to do good, to be rich in good deeds, and to be generous and willing to share. In this way they will lay up treasure for themselves as a firm foundation for the coming age, so that they may take hold of the life that is truly life.

Giving to those who minister to us

Philippians 4:10-19

I rejoice greatly in the Lord that at last you have renewed your concern for me. Indeed, you have been concerned, but you had no opportunity to show it. I am not saying this because I am in need, for I have learned to be content whatever the circumstances. I know what it is to be in need, and I know what it is to have plenty. I have learned the secret of being content in any and every situation, whether well fed or hungry, whether living in plenty or in want. I can do everything through him who gives me strength. Yet it was good of you to share in my troubles. Moreover, as you Philippians know, in the early days of your acquaintance with the gospel, when I set out from Macedonia, not one church shared with me in the matter of giving and receiving, except you only; for even when I was in Thessalonica, you sent me aid again and again when I was in need. Not that I am looking for a gift, but I am looking for what may be credited to your account. I have received full payment and even more; I am amply supplied, now that I have received from Epaphroditus the gifts you sent. They are a fragrant offering, an acceptable sacrifice, pleasing to God. And my God will meet all your needs according to his glorious riches in Christ Jesus.

Galatians 6:6-10

Anyone who receives instruction in the word must share all good things with his instructor. Do not be deceived: God cannot be mocked. A man reaps what he sows. The one who sows to please his sinful nature, from that nature will reap destruction; the one who sows to please the Spirit, from the Spirit will reap eternal life. Let us not become weary in doing good, for at the proper time we will reap a harvest if we do not give up. Therefore, as we have opportunity, let us do good to all people, especially to those who belong to the family of believers.

1 Timothy 5:17-18

The elders who direct the affairs of the church well are worthy of double honor, especially those whose work is preaching and teaching. For the Scripture says, "Do not muzzle the ox while it is treading out the grain," and "The worker deserves his wages."

Giving to meet the needs of your own family members

1 Timothy 5:8

If anyone does not provide for his relatives, and especially for his immediate family, he has denied the faith and is worse than an unbeliever.

Author's Testimony on Tithing

It all started with a dime. I grew up in a pastor's home and remember thinking my dad came up with the idea of "tithing" as a way of paying for the bills at the church. I had no idea it was a supernatural transaction with Almighty God and was the only way we could "get under the spout where all God's blessings come out" (Malachi 3:8-12).

It was in the second grade when I began to finally understand what my father was teaching me about tithing: that a dime out of every dollar belonged to God. It was a tithe (10%) that belonged to God, and when we went to church on Sunday to worship, everyone brought the tithe, from that week's income, to give to God. In those early years, even though I didn't fully understand the concept, I believed every person who called himself or herself a Christian was a tither. It wouldn't have entered my mind to even consider not tithing.

As a teenager, I tithed 10% of my income, every week, from mowing yards and then, from my first "real" job as a janitor at an apartment complex. In college, I tithed to the local church where I was a member. (Even though some of my fellow students excused themselves from tithing because they were "in" Bible college or they'd say they were using "their tithe" to pay for their education. I never understood that explanation and still don't.)

When my wife and I got married in 1977, we tithed every week. Even when we were expecting our first child, in our first pastorate, and there were a number of weeks when I wouldn't get paid because the church treasurer told me they "just didn't have the money that week," we tithed. We still tithed faithfully even though there were weeks when we did it fearfully, not knowing where the money would come from to cover all our bills. Still, we trusted God to be true to His Word and, as He says, put Him to the "test" (Malachi 3:10).

Today, our testimony is we are one of the most blessed families on the earth. We have a beautiful home that's paid for. We have four of the most incredible children any parents could ever want; two daughters, and our son and daughter-in-law. Our vehicles are paid for, our kids' college educations are paid for, everything we have is paid for, and because of God's Word and His blessing, we will live that way the rest of our lives.

Without hesitation, the single most important factor in our personal financial success has been trusting and obeying God in the matter of tithing. It's the essential foundation for God's blessing upon anyone's finances. When it comes to tithing, our obedience determines our abundance. Our disobedience precludes it.

We tell others we are "dependently wealthy," because we are absolutely dependent upon God for everything we have, and He more than meets all of our needs. He has given us far more than we have ever given Him and blessed us in ways we never dreamed (Deuteronomy 8:18; 28:12; Proverbs 10:22; 11:24-25).

How has that happened for our family? We have decided to trust God and His Word and, to the best of our ability, manage the resources He gives us the way He says to do it.

The Bible says God "loves a cheerful giver" (2 Corinthians 9:7). Those who give should do so not because they have to or because they should, but rather, because they want to. A generous giver who discovered this joy was missionary and martyr, Jim Elliot, who said, "He is no fool who gives what he cannot keep to gain what he cannot lose."

I had no idea back in the second grade what God was going to do in my life and where He was going to take me. Without question, He has "opened the floodgates of heaven" in my life and the lives of my family. And to think it all started with a dime.

By the way, we're still tithing every week to our local church and will until the day we die. Years ago we moved beyond the tithe to giving even more, and the blessings from that decision have been absolutely incredible.

If you haven't discovered the joy and blessing of tithing in your life yet, let me invite you to join me "under the spout where all of God's blessings come out."

Debt: The Real American Idol

Benjamin Franklin was an amazing man. He was one of the more remarkable founders of our great country. He helped frame our constitution, founded the first public library, and started the first fire station. He helped improve paving and lighting for streets, devised a way to reduce excessive smoking of chimneys, and invented the Franklin stove, which produced greater heat while requiring less fuel. He is probably best known for discovering electricity. Columnist Earl Wilson once said, "Franklin may have discovered electricity—but it was the man who invented the meter who made the money."

Benjamin Franklin was also known for his homespun wisdom. Although he lived in the 1700s, many of his sayings are still quoted today. For example, Franklin is credited with saying, "Keep your eyes open before marriage; half shut afterwards." He also said, "Well done is better than well said," "Fish and visitors smell in three days," and "The problem with doing nothing is not knowing when you're finished." He's also been credited with saying, "God helps those that help themselves," and "Early to bed, early to rise, makes a man healthy, wealthy and wise."

One of his lesser-known proverbs is: "Better to go to bed supperless, than wake up in debt." According to the *Wall Street Journal* (May 17, 2005), "one of his modern-day namesakes hasn't heeded the admonition." The man's name is Benjamin Franklin Baggett. He lives in Salt Lake City. Growing up, he was familiar with many of the witty sayings of Benjamin Franklin. His dad gave him several of Franklin's books, along with a Franklin memorial coin. But, unfortunately, the 38-year-old Benjamin Franklin Baggett didn't take it to heart. At least the part about the dangers of debt.

He received his first credit card on his honeymoon and immediately maxed it out. In 1995, he moved into the posh, tree-lined Harvard-Yale neighborhood close to the University of Utah that is home to a number of professors, attorneys, and doctors. He furnished the home with many of the same things his neighbors had, but used credit cards to do it. According to the article, Mr. Baggett said, "I felt insecure; I was an hourly-paid worker in this fancy neighborhood." He "was making $13 an hour for a time doing back-office work at a local bank while supporting two children." Twice he used a home-equity loan to pay off his credit card debts, and twice he ran up steep credit card bills again. When his debts reached $30,000 and he ran out of home equity, he filed for bankruptcy in 2003. "We came to rely on credit as part of our income, even though it wasn't part of our income," says Mr. Baggett. "I looked at $1,000 on my credit card as disposable income." Today, he no longer lives in that home. He had to sell it and he's divorced.

Proverbs 22:7 says, "The rich rule over the poor, and the borrower is servant to the lender." Verses 26 and 27 go on to say, "Do not be a man who strikes hands in pledge or puts up security for debts; if you lack the means to pay, your very bed will be snatched from under you."

I can't count the number of people I personally know who've been destroyed by the American idol of debt. Too many of us spend money we don't have, trying to keep up with people we don't even know or like, mortgaging a future we won't be able to enjoy because of a past we'd like to forget, and that's why our present stinks. We ignore the inevitable and disregard the proverbial wisdom and warnings of both the Bible and Benjamin Franklin.

Idolatry has always had a huge downside, especially the idol of debt. Benjamin Franklin said, "Money never made a man happy yet, nor will it. There is nothing in its nature to produce happiness. The more a man has, the more he wants. Instead of filling a vacuum, it makes one."

An article in the *San Francisco Chronicle* (May 20, 2005) warned of a new phenomenon in the world of what I call "dumb debt." Evidently, one of the hottest new ways to finance a home in California is with an "interest-only" loan. You don't pay anything on the principal. You only pay interest. According to the article, "Two out of three Bay Area home buyers are choosing interest-only loans, and some experts warn that the popularity of the controversial form of mortgage debt is a sign that the overheated housing market is boiling over . . . housing experts warn that these loans are loaded with risk . . . if home prices flatten or fall, borrowers could end up owing more than the home is worth."

If you're in debt today, take some incredibly wise advice—do whatever you have to do to start getting out of debt and start today! Benjamin Franklin said, "Never put off till tomorrow that which you can do today." The Bible says, "Better a little with the fear of the Lord than great wealth with turmoil" (Proverbs 15:16). Benjamin Franklin put it this way, "Better to go to bed supperless, than wake up in debt."

When it comes to debt, if you ignore the wisdom of the Bible and even Ben Franklin . . . you're in for a shock!

"TWENTY ONE DAYS"

by Pastor Barry L. Cameron

Jack Hyles, former pastor of the famous First Baptist Church of Hammond, Indiana, loved boxing. I remember years ago, listening to one of his sermons and hearing him talk about boxing. This isn't an exact quote, but it's close: "I think boxing is one of the most disgusting, barbaric, inhumane sports in the history of man. It's bloody, it's uncivilized, it's dangerous and it's deadly . . . but as long as they keep showing it on TV I intend to watch it." He obviously loved boxing.

I've never loved boxing like Dr. Hyles. But I do agree with everything else he said about it and yes, I've watched a few fights in my lifetime. Names like Muhammad Ali, George Foreman, Larry Holmes, Sugar Ray Leonard, Thomas "Hit Man" Hearns, Mike Tyson, and Evander Holyfield come to mind among the fighters I've seen battling in the boxing ring. (Which is actually a square, but they call it a ring.)

You may remember a boxer name Riddick Bowe. I don't remember a lot about him or his style, but I remember he won the undisputed heavyweight championship of the world defeating Evander Holyfield, back in November of 1992. Something else I remember about Riddick Bowe took place five years later in 1997. This time he wasn't in a boxing ring – he was in boot camp. Instead of trading punches he was facing the rigorous, regimented lifestyle of the U.S. Marine Corps. He had signed up for three months of boot camp in the pursuit of fulfilling his dream of being a Marine. However, three days later . . . Riddick Bowe quit. THREE DAYS! When he left he told his drill instructor and battalion commander "he couldn't handle the regimented training lifestyle." He was also quoted as saying, "I have a lot of respect for what recruits go through to become Marines."

Three days is a weekend – that's all – a weekend. You can't become a Marine in a weekend. You can become a quitter, and that's what many people do. They make New Year's resolutions resolving to do things differently. But, in a matter of days they've already quit. In fact, some folks quit so fast they make Riddick Bowe look like the marathon man.

The fact is, most experts agree it takes twenty-one days to develop a habit. That habit may take weeks, months or even years before it ultimately pays off. But the critical point for your success is those first twenty-one days. If you can stay at it until you've formed the habit, you're half way to the finish line. Because the right habit – once you have it – will have you and will carry you the rest of the way. However, if you quit in three days . . . well, all you have is a weak end.

If you want to get in the habit of eating right, guess how long you need to eat right? Twenty-one days. If you want to get in the habit of getting adequate exercise every day and get back in shape, how long do you need to exercise? That's right. Twenty-one days. If you want to develop the right habits, getting your finances under control, how long do you suppose you need to exercise serious fiscal discipline? Yep. Twenty-one days. If you want to get in the habit of having a quiet time every day with the Lord? Twenty-one days. Whatever it is you want to accomplish, if you want to develop the right habits to get you there, it will take twenty-one days, minimum. You can't and won't develop the right kind of habits without the discipline of doing it for that period of time. Period.

So, as you begin this brand new year of 2006, what is it that more than anything else in the world you'd like to accomplish? You can do it if you're willing to do what's necessary to develop the right habits to get you there. It won't be easy and you can't take weekends off. That's what quitters do. Quitters are always focused on time off or quitting time. That's why success continually eludes them. Because of their unwillingness to pay the price, they are always looking at an unattainable prize, an unreachable goal or an unrealized dream. Why? Their bad habits keep them from the good things they desperately desire.

Don't let that happen to you. Rather than keep your eye on the clock, keep your eye on the goal, the target, the dream you want to accomplish. To get there, you'll have to pay a price, most likely a high one, too, and you'll have to stay at it, every day – no matter what. But your persistence will pay off. Your discipline will bring dividends, and your commitment will translate into accomplishment.

Want some added motivation? Here it is: you want to know how far away you are from being a success? From seeing your dreams come true? From finally achieving those goals that have always seemed to somehow elude you?

Just twenty-one days!

© 2005 Barry L. Cameron

"He who ignores discipline comes to poverty and shame, but whoever heeds correction is honored."

(Proverbs 13:18)

"WHERE'S THE BEEF?"

by Pastor Barry L. Cameron

Dave Thomas and the folks at Wendy's restaurants popularized the phrase, *"Where's The Beef?"* several years ago in a very clever marketing campaign that yielded tremendous results. Restaurants and companies all over the world tried to come up with similar slogans that would bring similar success. At least in the hamburger business, none really came that close.

Several months ago, the Wendy's organization had to mount another marketing campaign. But this time it wasn't to promote their hamburgers. Rather, it was to save them. Instead of *"Where's The Beef?"* you might call this most recent effort, *"Where's The Finger?"* The people at Wendy's, specifically a Wendy's restaurant in San Jose, California, were trying to find out where a finger came from that showed up in a bowl of chili.

The story quickly spread all over the world and the Wendy's organization found themselves the butt of all the late night talk shows. But it was anything but funny to the No. 3 fast-food chain in America.

CEO, Jack Schuessler, estimated the loss to Wendy's as being 2.5% of sales or about $15 million from March 23rd through the end of April. He went on to say, "Besides that, it's the pride you have in your company. These were independent franchisees that got caught in the middle. The employees had fewer hours because of fewer sales. These people were victims. It's a shame in today's society how this incident gets blown up and really out of proportion."

This month, a couple from Nevada pleaded guilty to all the charges against them, admitting they had conspired to plant a human finger in a bowl of Wendy's chili in an attempt to extort money from the fast-food chain. The woman who made the false claim faces a maximum of almost ten years in prison. Her husband could get up to thirteen years. The woman had gone so far as to appear on ABC's *Good Morning America*, telling her story of finding the finger in her chili. Problem is, that's all it was: a story. She'd made it up. But just her claim alone did damage to hundreds, if not thousands of people, and affected the Wendy's organization in a totally unfair but completely unavoidable scandal that they are still recovering from today.

What's the lesson for us? What can and should those of us in the church learn from this? Can the body of Christ benefit from what happened to the folks in the burger business? I think so. Because there are countless numbers of churches and Christian organizations who have been scandalized and marginalized over the years by nothing more than stories. Stories concocted by people with agendas other than the Lord's and the resulting devastation is not sales, but souls.

Solomon warned, "The first to present his case seems right, till another comes forward and questions him" (Proverbs 18:17). In other words, don't believe everything you hear and always make sure to get all the facts before you respond in any way. It might even be you don't even need to respond. Not everyone who has a story to tell has anything more than just a "story" to tell.

We need to keep our eyes open for the finger-pointers and the finger-planters among us. Because more often than not, the beef those people bring to the table is their own.

© 2005 Barry L. Cameron

"DEATH-DEFYING DISCIPLINE"

by Pastor Barry L. Cameron

Everyone possesses it. So why don't we practice it? One simple reason: We don't have to. In fact, research shows a majority of us are constantly pursuing the exact opposite. We are an undisciplined lot and there are a lot of us.

In his new book, *"The Best Question Ever,"* Andy Stanley says, "There is something out there somewhere that has the ability to get your attention." But the truth is, until it does, most of us will keep pushing the limits, living on the edge, doing whatever we want to do – whenever we want to do it – even if it's bad for us.

We eat too much and exercise too little. We take too many chances and make too many dangerous choices. We hang on with a death grip to habits that harm us and hinder our witness for Christ. (Read that again, slowly.) We live life as if there is no tomorrow not even considering the fact we are radically altering and permanently affecting our tomorrows by a lack of discipline today.

All of us possess death-defying discipline. But few practice it . . . because we don't have to . . . at least not yet. Andy Stanley says, "Most Americans eat so unhealthily. It's not just a lack of discipline. Americans haven't really faced up to the reality of what the foods they eat are doing to their bodies. How do I know? Because I've seen how quickly the diet changes once someone has had a brush with cancer or heart disease. Lumps, clogs, and shortness of breath force a person to face up to what he or she has refused to acknowledge for years. And the revelation leads to death-defying discipline."

He goes on to say, "Bankruptcy can have the same effect. So can an unwanted pregnancy, a letter from your spouse's attorney, a DUI, or a trip to detox with one of your kids. And perhaps that's what it will take. There is something out there somewhere that has the ability to get your attention. Unfortunately, that something may scar you as well as scare you. You may be left with limited options and reduced opportunities. So why let things go that far?"

Why? Because most people have decided to keep doing what they want to do for the time being and only do what they have to do and ought to do when they finally have to do it. But they're not doing it right now, thank you, at least not until they have to. That's a colossal, and most often, very costly mistake.

Many times when we finally make the right decision, and begin to do what's right, it's already too late. Sometimes our situations and circumstances can't be turned around. Sometimes we let things go too far and go on too long so even the best medicines and most gifted physicians can't help us. The Bible warns, *"Anyone, then, who knows the good he ought to do and doesn't do it, sins"* (James 4:17).

You and I already possess the discipline to eat the right foods and eat the right amount. We possess the discipline to exercise daily and get back into shape. We have the ability to discipline ourselves, and control our spending, our anger, our tongue, you name it. We have the capacity and capability to be on time for work every day and to be the best employee in the office. We can successfully manage our money, contribute something to savings, prepare for retirement, and be a faithful tither every week if we really want to. All of us.

It just takes discipline . . . and you already possess it. You can do anything you set your heart and mind to do, anytime you want, any place you want. But you have to want to do it. Paul told Timothy we have a God-given "spirit of power, love and self-discipline" (2 Timothy 1:7). So why don't we put that discipline, that death-defying, God-given discipline to work on our behalf, right now?

Surely you're not going to wait until you have to . . .

© 2005 Barry L. Cameron

The Financial Freedom Workbook

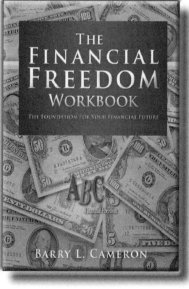

$6

The *Financial Freedom Workbook* is a tremendous tool to help you get on the road to financial freedom. In this 6-week study (perfect for small groups or individuals) you'll learn how to achieve complete financial freedom, pay off all your debts early, develop a simple, useable budget, find money you didn't know you had to put in savings each week, and how you can live an abundant life and pass it on to your children.

You can order workbooks from *The Disciple Shop* bookstore at Crossroads: 1.888.360.7648

To contact the author:
Barry L. Cameron, Senior Pastor
Crossroads Christian Church
6450 S. State Highway 360
Grand Prairie, TX 75052
or
www.crossroadschristian.net

To receive Barry's blog each week:
http://www.crossroadschristian.net/blog/